FOCUS ON

ROCKS & FOSSILS

RAY OLIVER

HAMLYN

ACKNOWLEDGEMENTS

Many of the photographs in this book were specially taken for Reed Children's Books by David Johnson. The publisher would like to thank the author, and Dr Robert Symes and Mr Alan Hart of the Department of Mineralogy at the Natural History Museum, Exhibition Road, London SW7, for their invaluable assistance in supplying the equipment and specimens for photography; and the following individuals and organizations for providing the photographs used in this book:
Ancient Art and Architecture Collection 44 bottom left, /B. Norman 32 (bottom). Ardea London Ltd 57 top. Bridgeman Art Library 47 top left, /John Bethell 22 top. Paul Brierley 59 bottom right. Bruce Coleman Ltd /Alfred Pasieka 59 top left, /Fritz Prenzel 71 centre left, /Michel Viard 44 bottom centre. Collections /Brian Shuel 46 left. Geoscience Features Picture Library 17 centre, 19 top right, 21 bottom, 22 bottom right, 39 bottom, 47 top right, 50 centre, 50 bottom left, 50 bottom centre, 50 bottom right, 51 top left, 51 top centre, 51 top right, 51 bottom left, 51 bottom right, 52 bottom, 59 top right, 67 bottom left, 67 bottom centre, 67 bottom right, 68 top, 69 top, 73 top. Michael Holford 28 bottom. Imagine 29 bottom left, 29 bottom right. Images Colour Library 58 left, 71 top. Frank Lane Picture Agency 16 top, /A.R. Hamblin 66 left, /Steve McCutcheon 25 bottom right, /M. Nimmo 29 top, /Peter Reynolds 20 centre, /Walther Rohdich 48 top left. © Arthur Montes De Oca 20 top. Natural History Museum, London 55 top, 56 left, 56-57 centre, 56-57 bottom, 57 bottom right, 70-71, 71 centre right. Reed International Books Ltd/David Johnson 8 top, 10-11, 12-13, 12 bottom left, 14-15, 16 left, 17 right, 18-19, 21 left, 22-23, 26-27, 30-31 bottom, 32-33, 32 bottom, 34-35, 37 right, 38 bottom, 40-41, 46-47, 60-61, 65, 66 right, 68 centre, 69 bottom, 72-73, 74 bottom. Rida Photo Library / David Bayliss 22 bottom left, 38 top, 52 top left. RTZ Ltd 49 top left. Science Photo Library / Roberto de Gugliemo 62 left, /Manfred Kage 67 centre right, /J. Koivula 50 top, /Martin Land 19 top left, 52 top right, /Andrew McClenaghan 36 bottom, /Claude Nuridsany & Marie Perennou 67 top, / Philippe Plailly 64 left, /David Parker 53 bottom left, 64 right, 75 right, /Dr Morley Read 48 top right, /Sinclair Stammers 8 bottom, 51 centre right, 51 bottom right, 75 left, /David Taylor 36 bottom left. Sotheby's 68 bottom centre, 68 bottom right. © Sinclair Stammers 64 bottom. By courtesy of the Board of Trustees of the Victoria & Albert Museum /D.P.P. Naish 71 bottom right. Tony Waltham Geoslides 42 top, 43 bottom. © John S. Whiteley 44-45.

Illustrators:
David Ashby (Garden Studio):11, 12, 13 (left), 15, 17 (right), 20, 24 (right), 34, 35, 37, 41, 42, 43, 48, 49, 53, 60-61 (top), 61 (right), 62-62. Peter Bull Art: 9, 16-17 (centre), 19, 21, 23, 24 (left), 25, 30-31, 33, 44, 45, 54, 55, 59-59, 60 (left), 60-61 (bottom), 69.

Editor: Andrew Farrow
Designers: Anne Sharples, Mark Summersby
Series Designer: Anne Sharples
Production Controller: Linda Spillane
Picture Researcher: Caroline Hensman

First published in Great Britain 1993
by Hamlyn Children's Books,
an imprint of Reed Children's Books Limited,
Michelin House, 81 Fulham Road, London SW3 6RB,
and Auckland, Melbourne, Singapore and Toronto

Copyright © 1993 Reed International Books Limited

ISBN 0 600 57368 0

A CIP catalogue record for this book is available
at the British Library

Printed in Great Britain

CONTENTS

Minerals, Rocks and Fossils 8
Equipment 10
Working at Home 14
Igneous Rocks 16
Sedimentary Rocks 18
Metamorphic Rocks 22
Movements in the Earth 24
Finding Rocks 26
Making a Survey 30
Properties of Minerals 32
Flame Tests 36
Mineral Data 38
Silica 40
Mineral Waters 42
Metals From the Rocks 44
The Most Important Metal 46
Extract Your Own Metals 48
Fossils: An Amazing Variety 50
How Old Are They? 54
Making Your Name 56
Fossils and Oil 58
Crystals 60
Growing Crystals 62
Crystals Around Us 66
Diamonds are Forever 68
Storage and Display 72
Advancing Your Hobby 74
Index 76

MINERALS, ROCKS AND FOSSILS

Collecting minerals, rocks and fossils is a great way to learn about the natural world. It is one of the few areas of science where amateurs still make important discoveries. If you study rocks and fossils you will be finding out about the materials from which the Earth is made, and also about the history of the Earth.

MINERALS

Minerals are naturally-occurring substances, such as quartz or diamond. Each mineral is made up of lots of particles. In most minerals, these particles are arranged in a regular order, forming crystals (see page 60). Although they, too, form crystals, plant- or animal-based substances such as sugar are not minerals.

Quartz is a common mineral in the Earth's crust. Quartz is found in several forms: as sand on the beach, as gemstones such as purple amethyst, and also as flint in chalk rock.

ROCKS

Rocks are made of minerals, rather as walls are made of bricks. Some rocks contain only one mineral, all the 'bricks' being the same. Chalk is like this. The only mineral present is called calcium carbonate. However, most rocks are mixtures of two or more different minerals. For example, granite contains the three minerals quartz, mica and feldspar.

Rocks form very slowly, often needing millions of years. An exception is the rock that is formed by an erupting volcano. Huge amounts of liquid volcanic rock, called lava, can be released in just hours or days.

WHAT ABOUT FOSSILS?

Fossils are the remains of things that were alive thousands or millions of years ago. Sometimes fossils are still formed of their original material, such as sharks' teeth or shells. Usually the remains have been changed chemically, or fossilized. This means

Granite is a rock made of three different minerals. The glassy mineral is quartz, the black specks are mica and the largest crystals are feldspar.

granite

quartz

mica

feldspar

that the original bones or leaves have been replaced by minerals such as quartz. Sometimes only an impression of the creature's shape is left in the rocks: this is called a fossil print or cast. The preserved footprints of dinosaurs are regarded as fossils.

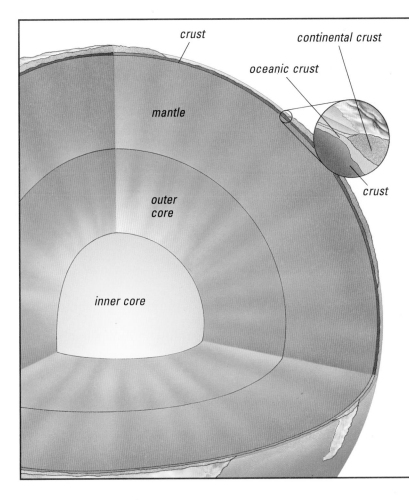

crust

continental crust

oceanic crust

mantle

outer core

inner core

crust

UNDER THE SURFACE

Nobody is certain what the inside of the Earth is like. However, scientists believe that it is made of layers, like an egg.

In the centre is the inner core, which is surrounded by the outer core and mantle. Although the inner core is very hot - about 3,000°C - the great pressure of the material around it stops it melting. The rock melts only when the pressure is relieved. Then the molten rock, or magma, tries to rise through cracks in the rock around it. If it reaches the surface - perhaps through a volcano - the magma cools, and minerals 'freeze' out of the molten rock, forming crystals. Eventually the rock solidifies, too.

The outer layer is the crust - and it's as thin as an eggshell compared to the Earth's size! The crust is broken into huge sections called plates. Some areas of these plates are oceanic crust - the sea floor - while others are the continental crust, the land masses. Where these plates meet, the intense heat and pressure inside the Earth is revealed, and most of the world's volcanoes and earthquakes occur.

This is a collection of beautifully-preserved ammonites (left). Ammonites were molluscs, related to nautiluses and squids, that lived beneath the sea between 65 and 400 million years ago. You can often find them in marine rocks.

COLLECTING ROCKS AND FOSSILS

Rock and fossil collecting is a fascinating hobby. You can go hunting for specimens, carry out experiments, and learn how rocks, minerals and fossils are formed. It's a good idea to join a club or society, because the other members will share your enthusiasm and help you learn more about your hobby. In many towns and cities there are natural history or archaeological societies, often with a junior section. At a club you may find out about mail-order dealers, rock shops or good places to look for specimens. There will also be field trips to interesting sites.

READ ALL ABOUT IT

This book is all about collecting and studying rocks and fossils. First you'll find out about equipment and how to use it. Then there are sections on types of rocks and and how to find them. It also tells you about the many fascinating properties of minerals, how to test and identify them, and looks in detail at mineral waters, mining and metals. There are also sections on fossils and dinosaurs, on the hundreds of crystals that can be found all around us, and on the fabulous world of gemstones and jewellery. Finally, the book shows you how to display your collection, and then suggests ways in which you can develop your hobby. Whether you want to hunt for specimens, or just like to read about them, we hope that you find this book useful. The most important thing is that you enjoy yourself. If you find a rare specimen, you may even become famous as well!

EQUIPMENT

You can start collecting rocks and fossils with nothing more complicated than a plastic bag to hold any pebbles that you find. The serious collector will need more equipment than this, though you may already have many items around your home.

HAMMER

Every serious collector will need a strong hammer. The best type will have a square end for striking rocks and a pickaxe end to lever out specimens. There's no need to buy a huge hammer - get one that's not too heavy for you to hold properly.

MAP AND COMPASS

A large-scale map of the area will help you find your way, and allow you to record the best locations for future trips. A compass will not only give you directions but can be used to detect magnetic minerals, too.

CHISELS AND BRUSH

A strong masonry chisel is useful to split rock layers apart. You will find that some rocks split more easily in one direction, like chopping wood along the grain. Often you can find fossils like this, hidden and squashed between the rock layers. A set of small chisels or a metal spike may loosen the rock around the fossil. Some rocks are so soft that you can use a soft brush or an old toothbrush to clean around the fossils. A penknife is useful for carefully freeing crystals or fossils from rock.

NOTEBOOK AND PENCIL

Once you have a sample you will need to describe it and note where it was found. Take a notebook and pencil to record your finds, because it is very easy to forget important details at the end of a long day in the field.

STURDY CLOTHES

Safety glasses or goggles are essential to protect your eyes from rock splinters. A hard hat is necessary if you are working near a cliff face: quarry owners will insist that you wear a safety hat before granting permission to visit. Always wear warm clothes and a pair of sturdy shoes or boots.

CHIPPING AND HAMMERING

If you can't remove a sample by scraping with a chisel or spike, you'll need to use a hammer. Use only as much force as necessary to split the rock or you will damage the sample. You may need to support the rock you are hammering so that it doesn't fall away - and be careful not to hit your hand! *Always* wear safety glasses when hammering so that chips don't get into your eyes.

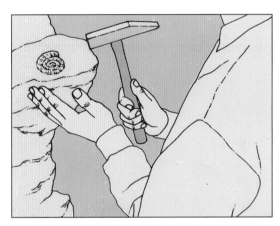

Always hammer gently at first when trying to separate a specimen from rock. If possible, chip away from the specimen, so that you won't damage it if your chisel slips. Take your time so that you don't make mistakes: a fossil will have been waiting millions of years for you to find it!

Carefully trim unwanted material from the edges of the sample before packing it ready to take home. Leave any final chipping or trimming to size until you get home. One blow that is too hard can split the whole sample.

SIEVING

 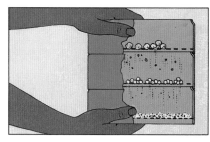 

Nests of sieves are used for sorting loose material into grains of the same size. Put the nest of sieves together and add a spadeful of the crushed mixture to the top sieve.

Shake the nest gently to separate the mixture according to the size of the particles. The different size meshes in the sieves will hold back particles that are too large to go through their holes.

Remove each sieve and tip its contents onto some newspaper so you can examine it with a hand lens. You may need to crush large pieces and sieve them again.

BAGS AND CONTAINERS

The easiest way to wrap specimens safely is to use sheets of newspaper, remembering to put in a label with each sample. Use a strong bag to carry your samples: rocks are very heavy! Canvas bags, of the type that you can buy in army surplus stores, are ideal. Other plastic containers, such as empty margarine tubs, can be used to hold sands and other smaller specimens that won't break easily. Don't use glass containers, which might break while you are scrambling around.

SAFETY FIRST!
When you see this symbol on one of the following pages, ask an adult to help you with the experiment or activity described. Always wear safety glasses and protective gloves when using acid or a naked flame, or when chipping rock.

SIEVES AND TROWEL

Clay or sand can be sieved with a kitchen flour sieve to remove small fossils for examination. You can buy nests of sieves where each one has smaller mesh holes than the next. Different sizes of material collect in each sieve and can be examined separately. A trowel is particularly useful for digging in gravel and loose rock.

WRAPPING SAMPLES

Place the specimen near one corner of a sheet of newspaper, delicate side up.

Carefully fold the sides of the newspaper over the specimen.

Roll up the newspaper, keeping it neatly and firmly together.

Tuck a label in the package and put it in your bag.

FIELD SKETCHES

You will not be able to take away some of the samples you find. To keep a record of them, make a field sketch using a pencil and squared paper. Draw the sample from more than one angle and put a scale on your drawings. Include every detail that could help you identify the sample later, such as colour and texture. When you get home compare your sketch with reference books. Or you could make a sketch map of your local area, marking on it the types of building stones you can find.

Ammonite replaced by calcite. Found partly embedded in limestone. 27 July 1992 Crow cliffs

5cm

WORKING AT HOME

Some of the most interesting work on rocks, minerals and fossils can be carried out at home. For example, you may want to identify a mineral sample by testing its properties, or separate a fossil completely from its surrounding rock. For these investigations, and others described in this book, some more specialized equipment is needed. Do not use equipment that will later be used to prepare food.

G-CLAMP
A G-clamp (right) is useful for holding samples firmly in place while you trim them. Always prepare a good working area for testing and working on specimens.

MEASURING EQUIPMENT
You'll need some scales to weigh your samples for density tests (see page 35). Ordinary kitchen scales (below) will be accurate enough for large specimens. A small measuring jug with a scale is perfect for measuring the volume of a sample - the plastic cylinders (right) used by photographers to measure chemical solutions are ideal.

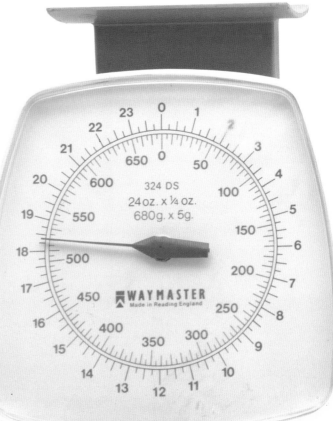

MAGNIFYING GLASS
If you have a magnifying glass or microscope, you can really look at the fine details of your specimens. A pocket hand lens is useful for studying specimens in the field.

ACID

A bottle of weak acid is needed for removing rock (right) and fizz tests (see page 34). Only carry out these tests in the presence of an adult. The most suitable acids are ethanoic acid (acetic acid) in vinegar, or dilute hydrochloric acid. Acids are corrosive, so always wear safety glasses and rubber gloves.

REMOVING ROCK

Acids can be used to dissolve away limestone (carbonate) rock to release fossils found in them. Protect each fossil with a layer of clear nail polish because some fossils, too, will dissolve in acid.

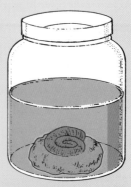

Carefully paint the exposed parts of the fossil with clear nail polish. Wait until the polish hardens.

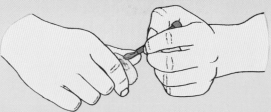

Place the sample in weak acid and leave it in a safe and well ventilated place for a day. Do not seal the container.

Using protective gloves and safety glasses, carefully rinse the acid from the sample using lots of running water. If necessary, repeat all these steps until the fossil is free of the rock.

BOOKS

Books are essential for identifying specimens. A well-illustrated field guide will describe and show many types of rocks, minerals and fossils. Local guide books may also have some useful information about interesting geological features in the area.

IGNEOUS ROCKS

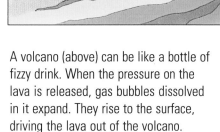

There are three types of rock in the Earth's crust: igneous, sedimentary and metamorphic rocks. The earliest to form were the primary, or igneous, rocks. Igneous rocks are formed at high temperatures. They are still forming today, one example being the lava that flows from a volcano.

Igneous rocks can be recognized by their crystals. When they cool quickly they can form obsidian. Slow-cooling gabbro has large crystals, whilst basalt lava is in between.

basalt

obsidian

gabbro

A volcano (above) can be like a bottle of fizzy drink. When the pressure on the lava is released, gas bubbles dissolved in it expand. They rise to the surface, driving the lava out of the volcano.

TYPES OF IGNEOUS ROCK

When lava escapes from a volcano it loses its heat quite quickly and sets solid. There isn't much time for any crystals to grow in the cooling lava flow. You can recognize lavas because they often look glassy with few, if any, obvious crystals. The crystals are there but they are very small. Sometimes the lava will have lots of holes in it where gases bubbled out of the molten rock. One of the commonest lavas cools to form the rock basalt, which is often black. You may need to use a hand lens to find any crystals in basalt.

Not all igneous rocks escape at the Earth's surface like lavas. Most igneous rocks are formed deep underground, where the rocks above trap the heat like a blanket. Rocks that cool underground take a long time to set solid. This means that these sorts of igneous rocks have larger crystals than volcanic rocks. The best known example is granite, a very hard rock. Although it is formed underground, granite can be seen at the Earth's surface because the rocks above it wear away over millions of years.

LAVA FLOWS

Different types of lava flow downhill away from a volcano at different speeds. Some lavas are thick, or viscous, and flow slowly. Being quite thick, they sometimes block the escape of gas from the volcano, causing a build-up of gas. When the pressure gets very great, the volcano erupts violently. Other lavas are very hot and runny, and will flow a long way. They usually cool to form basalt.

When magma is very hot and under pressure it forces its way to the surface. If there is a weak spot in the crust the magma escapes and a volcano forms (left). Some lavas can spread for miles, causing great destruction (below right).

Pumice (above) is formed in volcanic eruptions. It is often light enough to float on water.

ROCKHOUND'S HINT
Many igneous rocks are very hard and can be polished to an attractive finish. Look for their use in buildings and monuments.

OTHER IGNEOUS ROCKS

Granites are light-coloured rocks, because they contain pale-coloured feldspar crystals. Some igneous rocks are much darker than granite. One example is gabbro which is also much heavier than a similarly-sized piece of granite - gabbro is more dense than granite.

You may have a piece of igneous rock in your bathroom, for scraping away dirt. It is pale-coloured, very light for its size and full of bubbles. It may even float in water. This rock is called pumice, and is formed by some types of volcano.

LAVA FLOWS

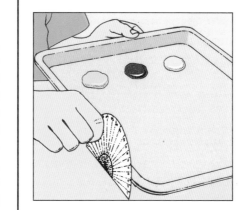

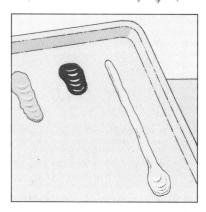

Add some separate pools of different liquids along one edge of a metal baking tray. Try syrup, treacle and cooking oil as your examples of lava. Slowly raise the edge of the tray to start the liquids flowing down the slope. You can measure the angle of the slope using a protractor.

Which is the most viscous liquid? It will be the most sticky one, the one which flows most slowly down the slope. You can also investigate the effect of temperature on lava flows. Cool the liquids in a fridge and then try them again to see if there is a difference in speed of flow.

SEDIMENTARY ROCKS

When igneous rocks are worn away by the weather they form sedimentary rocks. These are made of pieces of other rocks - they are secondhand rocks. They contain grains of material held together by different kinds of natural cement. The grains often show a pattern, or bands running through them. Some special sedimentary rocks are made of shells of sea creatures or even of salt layers.

sandstone

chalk

STRATA

As rocks wear away, the pieces are carried by wind or water until they settle. Often the material reaches the sea where it settles in layers on the sea bed. Large and heavy pieces settle quite quickly. Tiny pieces of sand or fine mud settle more slowly on the sea bed - they often travel many kilometres before settling. New layers, or strata, of sedimentary rock slowly form. Even under the weight of new layers above, it can take millions of years before the soft sand or mud turns into a hard sandstone or mudstone.

Can you guess what to look for when trying to identify a rock as being a sedimentary rock? One obvious clue is the presence of layers. Another strong clue is the presence of fossils in the rock. The shells of sea creatures fall to the sea bed when they die, and can be preserved as fossils in the newly-forming sedimentary rocks, such as limestone.

SANDSTONES

Sandstones are usually easy to recognize. They look as though beach sand has been glued together. You can often find sandstones used in buildings. If you look closely with a hand lens, you might see the shape of individual grains. Sandstones formed from desert sands have worn edges because the grains bumped together. Some sandstones formed in the sea have ripple marks in them, just like the marks of water ripples you can see on a beach.

algal limestone

conglomerate

mudstone

breccia

limestone

Sedimentary rocks form in similar ways, but they can look very different. In chalk the particles are so small that you can hardly see them. In a conglomerate the rounded pebbles can be very big.

Strata are layers of sedimentary rock. Most rock strata are horizontal when they are formed, as in the sandstone pictured above. However, violent earth movements can crush and bend rock strata into amazing patterns (left).

CHALK

Chalk is another common sedimentary rock. There is no other rock that can look so white. Chalk is a very pure form of limestone. The limestones come in several colours, yellow-white and grey being the most common. You may find lumps of the mineral flint, a much harder grey material, in chalk rock.

Other sedimentary rocks include mudstones and clays, which consist of fine particles. There are also rocks called conglomerates, made up of pebbles.

clay

COMPACTION AND CEMENTATION

As sediments settle on the sea bed their weight presses down on the layers below. This presses out water from the material and squeezes, or compacts, the particles together, forming sedimentary rock. There are several natural cements, such as silica in sandstones, and calcium carbonate in limestones, that stick particles together to make new rocks. The cement is left as a coating on the particles when water is squeezed out.

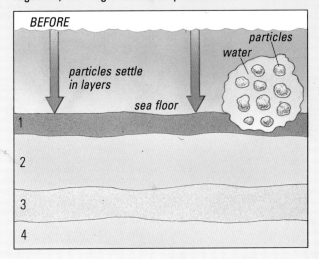

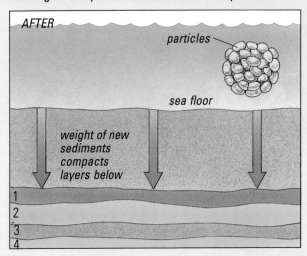

SALT DEPOSITS

Salt flats are a special type of sedimentary rock. They are formed when salt lakes and seas dry up, leaving shiny masses of crystals behind. This is what is happening at the moment in the Dead Sea in Israel. All over the world there are salt flats and lakes, as well as layers of salt underground. Salt flats provide ideal surfaces for attempts on the land speed record.

Salt is called an evaporite deposit since it is left behind when water evaporates. You can carry out an experiment to make your own salt deposit. Start by making up a very strong solution of salt by dissolving as much as you can in some water. Pour the salty water into a shallow tray of sand until all the sand is covered. Leave the water in a warm place to evaporate. When the sand has dried out, examine the salt layer. You may be able to see little cubes of salt - salt crystals. Look for patterns of cracks in the surface of the salt. These will probably look like the cracks you can find in real rocks. If you find salt crystals in a rock, it shows that the weather was very dry when that rock was formed long ago.

When water evaporates from a sea faster than it is replaced, the water dries up to leave salt flats (above). These are good places to speed test cars. Mud cracks form when mud dries out, and can be preserved as rocks (right) that show the original pattern of cracks.

RIPPLES ON THE BEACH

Use a large shallow tray for this experiment. Add a layer of sand about 1cm deep and then pour in enough water to cover the sand to a depth of 2cm. When the sand has settled again, move a ruler up and down to make a pattern of waves in the water. Look at the patterns that form in the sand and make a sketch. Try moving the ruler at different speeds to see if the pattern changes. You can find ripple marks just like these in sedimentary rocks, sometimes with preserved footprints as well.

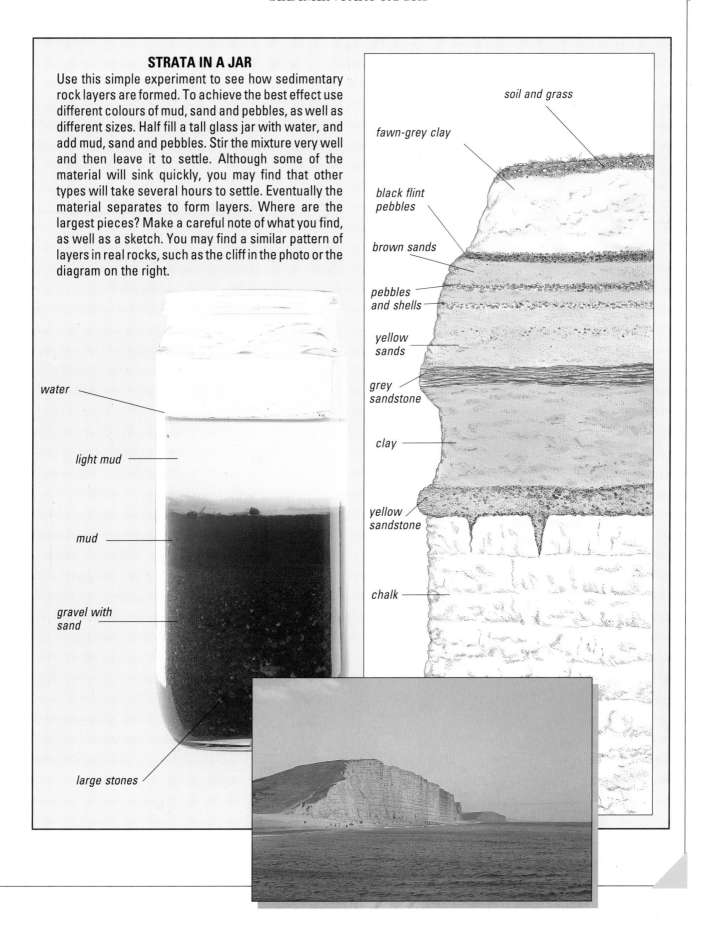

STRATA IN A JAR

Use this simple experiment to see how sedimentary rock layers are formed. To achieve the best effect use different colours of mud, sand and pebbles, as well as different sizes. Half fill a tall glass jar with water, and add mud, sand and pebbles. Stir the mixture very well and then leave it to settle. Although some of the material will sink quickly, you may find that other types will take several hours to settle. Eventually the material separates to form layers. Where are the largest pieces? Make a careful note of what you find, as well as a sketch. You may find a similar pattern of layers in real rocks, such as the cliff in the photo or the diagram on the right.

water

light mud

mud

gravel with sand

large stones

soil and grass

fawn-grey clay

black flint pebbles

brown sands

pebbles and shells

yellow sands

grey sandstone

clay

yellow sandstone

chalk

METAMORPHIC ROCKS

marble

All metamorphic rocks have been changed from other kinds of rock. The changes are usually caused by great heat within the Earth, or pressure from movements in the crust, or by both together. Just as soft clay can be fired in a kiln to form hard, brittle pottery, so rocks can be changed by metamorphism. You are unlikely to find fossils in metamorphic rocks because heat and pressure will have destroyed them.

SLATE

Slate, which is formed under great pressure under the Earth's surface, is one of the easiest metamorphic rocks to recognize. The great pressure pushes all the minerals inside the slate until they point in the same direction. This means that slate can be split into thin sheets, and for many years has been used for roofing.

When slate is split for roofing, much of the rock is broken and wasted. If you go to a slate quarry there will be plenty of samples for you to examine. Slate can be grey, green or even purple.

SCHIST

If the pressure and heat are very great the rock can change into a glittering new metamorphic rock called schist. This rock is usually bent into wavy layers, often containing shiny black mica crystals.

Sometimes you can find gemstones called garnets in schist. They are usually red and have been formed by changes to the original rock. These garnets are in mica schist.

Slates for roofing (below) are made by quarrying blocks of slate and then splitting them along the weakest planes in the rock. The best slate splits easily into flat sheets when a chisel is applied in the right place. The sheets can then be trimmed to the right size.

schist

metaquartzite

slate

gneiss

The Earth's rocks are naturally recycled over millions of years (right). Igneous rocks are broken down by weathering to form sedimentary rocks. These in turn can be changed into metamorphic rocks. Marble (left and below right) has been used for many years to decorate magnificent rooms and buildings.

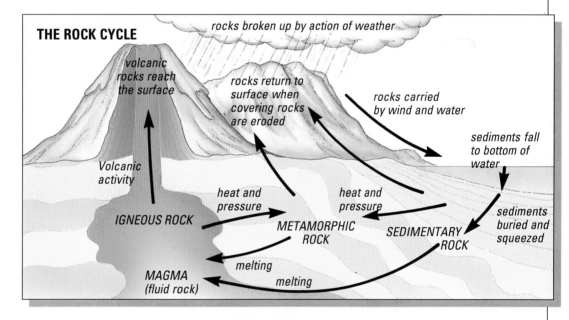

THE ROCK CYCLE

rocks broken up by action of weather

volcanic rocks reach the surface

rocks return to surface when covering rocks are eroded

rocks carried by wind and water

sediments fall to bottom of water

Volcanic activity

heat and pressure

heat and pressure

sediments buried and squeezed

IGNEOUS ROCK

METAMORPHIC ROCK

SEDIMENTARY ROCK

melting

MAGMA (fluid rock)

melting

MARBLE

This is the best-known metamorphic rock of them all. When limestones are heated and squeezed by metamorphic changes underground the result is marble. If the original limestone was very pure, the marble will be white, hard and have a sugary texture. Otherwise the impurities in the limestone produce beautiful colours and bands in the marble. The rock does not split easily and so must be mined very carefully. However, marble can be carved and polished and so has been a favourite material for sculptors for thousands of years. It is also broken into slabs and used for tiles and to decorate buildings.

MOVEMENTS IN THE EARTH

The surface of the Earth is changing all the time because of the movement of the crust. Also, the rocks of the Earth's crust are continually being built up, worn away and re-formed. These changes are usually very slow. Except for volcanic eruptions and earthquakes, most geological changes take much longer than one human lifetime.

MOUNTAINS

Mountains are the most prominent rock features of the Earth's crust. There are four main types of mountain. Some are built up as volcanoes, as molten igneous rock is forced up through a weak point in the crust. Many islands are the tops of underwater volcanoes. Other mountains are formed as pressure builds up beneath the surface, forcing it up to form huge mounds called dome mountains.

FOLDS

Movements of the Earth's crust can make the original horizontal layers buckle into folds. Anticlines are upward folds, synclines sag down.

faulted fold

FOLD MOUNTAINS

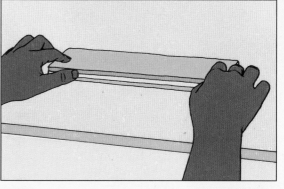

For this experiment, roll out some rectangular layers of plasticine of different colours. Put the layers on top of each other on a smooth surface. Each layer of plasticine represents a rock stratum.

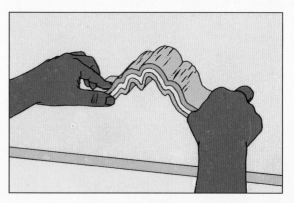

Next, hold opposite ends of the plasticine layers and push them towards each other. Note what happens as the mountain grows. As you push, stress is put on the layers and they may even split apart. You can try similar experiments with piles of blankets or even layers of jelly.

Sometimes, movement of the crust forces huge blocks of the crust to rise up and others to sink. This is how block mountains are formed. Block mountains often have flat tops, with flat-bottomed valleys between them. Other mountains are called fold mountains. They have curved layers of rock. Try the experiment above and you will find out how scientists believe fold mountains formed.

When the Earth's crust moves, huge forces push against the rocks. Under this great strain, the rocks try to move. Sometimes they bend or flow, producing folds (left), but sometimes they break, forming a fault (right). Try the experiments on these pages to show both types of rock movement.

EARTHQUAKE!

Support the ends of a pasta stick on some blocks so that the pasta looks like a bridge. Now start adding some weight to the centre of the pasta stick. Keep adding weight until something very noticeable happens - the stick snaps suddenly. Sometimes real rocks underground behave like this - they don't flow or bend like the ones in the plasticine experiment, but resist the strain until they break. When this happens there is an earthquake.

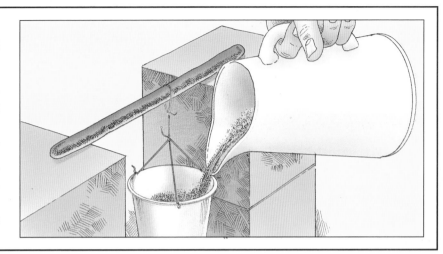

FAULTS

These are some of the types of fault that occur when rocks break.

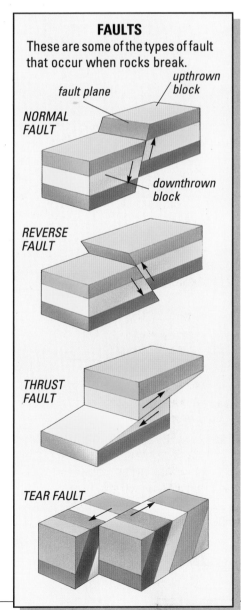

NORMAL FAULT

fault plane
upthrown block
downthrown block

REVERSE FAULT

THRUST FAULT

TEAR FAULT

Earthquakes usually happen without warning and last only a few seconds or minutes. The amount of energy released in an earthquake can be large enough to wreck buildings, destroy bridges and move roads. Modern buildings can be designed to withstand most earthquakes.

FINDING ROCKS

Before you start hunting for rocks and minerals, you need to know what to look for and where to go. Probably the best place to start looking for information is your school or local town library. Don't forget to look in the telephone book, which will have the addresses of local geological and industrial museums, as well as clubs and societies.

BUILDING A REFERENCE LIBRARY

It's not difficult to build up a good reference library you can use in your studies. As well as buying new books, ask for them as birthday presents, or look in secondhand bookshops. Local newspapers often run stories about finds made in the area, perhaps when the foundations of a new building or road are being dug. Cut these out and stick them in a scrapbook, together with any magazine articles that you find.

Tell friends about your hobby, and perhaps they will collect information for you. You could even take photographs of interesting rocks or buildings and add these to your scrapbook. It won't be long before you have a unique and valuable record to show other friends who share your hobby.

PHOTOGRAPHY

Photos can be an invaluable record of where you have found specimens. Take a general view of the surrounding landscape or building to show where the rock or decorative stonework is located. Next, take a close-up to show details of the specimen. You may find crystals, interesting colours or patterns.

Write down the details of the location, the date and a description of the subject. If your camera has adjustable settings, note the film speed, exposure and lighting conditions, too, so that you will know which settings give the best results.

A scrapbook can contain any information or pictures connected with your hobby.

A QUICK GUIDE TO ROCKS

This is a key to the guide on the next page. It shows how geologists define the different sizes of rock grains.

KEY

I = Igneous
M = Metamorphic
S = Sedimentary

Grain Size

Size (mm)	Name
Less than $\frac{1}{256}$	Clay
$\frac{1}{16}$ - $\frac{1}{256}$	Silt
2 - $\frac{1}{16}$	Sand
2 - 4	Gravel
4 - 64	Pebbles
And	
$\frac{1}{16}$ - $\frac{1}{8}$	Very Fine
$\frac{1}{8}$ - $\frac{1}{4}$	Fine
$\frac{1}{4}$ - $\frac{1}{2}$	Medium
$\frac{1}{2}$ - 1	Coarse
1 - 2	Very Coarse

ROCKHOUND'S HINT
Look at the stones in your own back garden - you might find something interesting. Some of them may have been brought there from another area.

A QUICK GUIDE TO ROCK IDENTIFICATION

The best way to learn how to identify rocks, minerals and fossils is to see as many examples as possible. Some museums will let you handle specimens, which is even better. The chart below will help you identify some of the most common types of rock. Simply follow the questions, answers and information supplied.

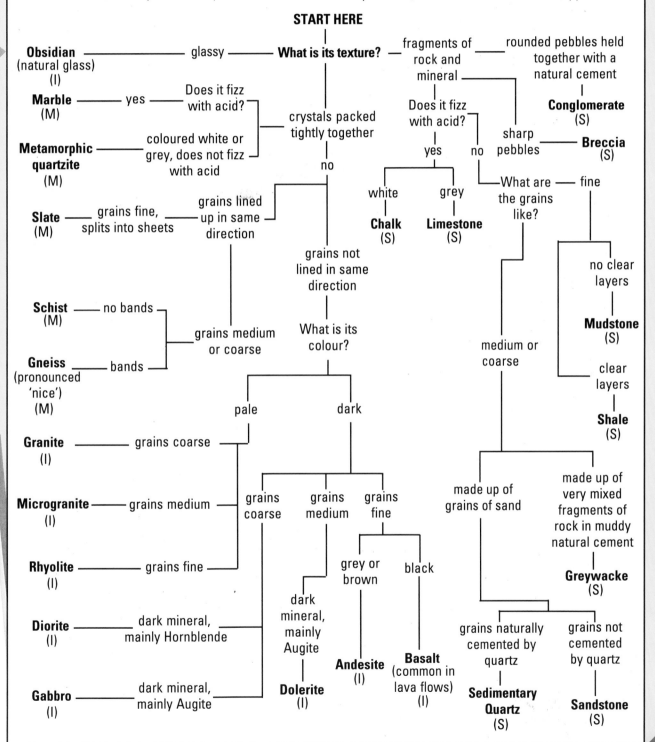

START HERE

Obsidian (natural glass) (I) — glassy — **What is its texture?**

fragments of rock and mineral — rounded pebbles held together with a natural cement — **Conglomerate** (S)

Marble (M) — yes — Does it fizz with acid?

Metamorphic quartzite (M) — coloured white or grey, does not fizz with acid

crystals packed tightly together

Does it fizz with acid? — yes — white — **Chalk** (S) / grey — **Limestone** (S)

no — sharp pebbles — **Breccia** (S)

no — What are the grains like? — fine

Slate (M) — grains fine, splits into sheets — grains lined up in same direction

grains not lined in same direction

no clear layers — **Mudstone** (S)

clear layers — **Shale** (S)

Schist (M) — no bands

Gneiss (pronounced 'nice') (M) — bands — grains medium or coarse

What is its colour?

medium or coarse

made up of grains of sand

made up of very mixed fragments of rock in muddy natural cement — **Greywacke** (S)

Granite (I) — grains coarse — pale / dark

Microgranite (I) — grains medium — grains coarse / grains medium / grains fine

Rhyolite (I) — grains fine

grey or brown — **Andesite** (I) / black — **Basalt** (common in lava flows) (I)

Diorite (I) — dark mineral, mainly Hornblende

dark mineral, mainly Augite — **Dolerite** (I)

grains naturally cemented by quartz — **Sedimentary Quartz** (S)

grains not cemented by quartz — **Sandstone** (S)

Gabbro (I) — dark mineral, mainly Augite

OUT AND ABOUT

As soon as you start collecting rocks and minerals, you will begin to notice examples of them all around you. If you live in a place where the houses are more than 50 years old, you may find that the kerbstones and street paving provide good examples to study. Ones made of granite are easy to recognize by the three types of crystal they contain. If the paving is dark coloured with few crystals, it is probably a volcanic rock. Modern kerbstones and paving stones are usually made of concrete or brick, which are artificial or 'man-made' rocks.

MAKING NOTES

Always keep a note when you see something of interest, such as the rock and soil layers in a cutting being dug for a new road. In this way you will build up a picture of the geology of your home area. Do not enter dangerous areas such as construction sites. If you know of an interesting building project, why not write to the building company to see if you can visit the site and talk to the engineer?

THE ROCKHOUND'S CODE

Never trespass on private property.

Ask permission before removing specimens.

Take only a small piece of specimens you find.

Don't go near cliff tops.

Always wear a safety hat when near cliffs.

Respect wildlife such as plants and nesting birds.

ROCKS ON BUILDINGS

Looking up from the pavement, you will see that shop and office fronts often include polished rock slabs for decoration. In some cases you will find fossils, which show that the rock is almost certainly a sedimentary rock. Churches and public buildings often have statues, or architectural decoration round the windows. These may be the types of stone that have been quarried locally. In some places all the older houses are built of stone, sometimes with stone tiles or slates on the roof.

AT THE CHURCH

A church is often one of the oldest buildings in a town. It is probably the best example of a building where rock has been used for construction and decoration. You may think that the graveyard is a depressing place, but there will be a good selection of rocks on display there. See if you can find out how quickly the different rock types used for headstones wear away in the wind and rain - the dates on the stones will help you make comparisons.

Look carefully at buildings to see the range of rocks used. There may be decorative marble, limestone around the windows, slate on the roof, granite or basalt paving in front, and limestone steps and carvings.

Quarries, such as this large sand quarry, are ideal for looking at fresh material before it has weathered. You may find fossils as well as the sand, clay or rock that is being extracted.

CLIFFS AND QUARRIES

The best places to find rocks are cliffs. They are dangerous places, and you should *never* go near them without an adult. Be careful when approaching cliffs, and avoid places where there have been landslips. Look for any warning signs. Most cliffs have clearly-marked routes to the beach. As you go down them, look for rock strata. On the beach you might find fossils and minerals that have been weathered out of the cliff face. Sand and pebbles are worth collecting, too.

When you find some specimens, take them and your collecting equipment to a safe distance from the cliff. You must *always* ask permission before removing specimens. Most land is private property. Also, many sites contain specimens that are protected by law, and you will be destroying part of the country's heritage by removing them.

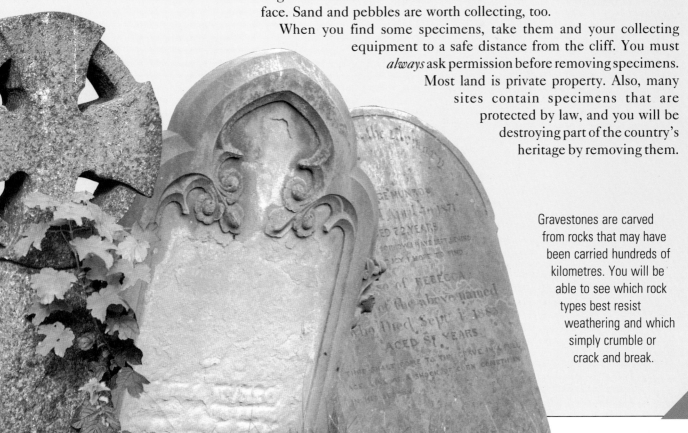

Gravestones are carved from rocks that may have been carried hundreds of kilometres. You will be able to see which rock types best resist weathering and which simply crumble or crack and break.

MAKING A SURVEY

YOUR OWN MAP

When you return from your survey, mark on the map where you found samples. Include a key to give the name or description of the sample. Mark any interesting building stones on your map. When you have finished you can keep the original map and your overlay together to give a permanent record.

Once you gain a greater knowledge of the rock types in your area, you may want to conduct a survey and make your own geological map. Don't be too ambitious at first - choose a small area close to home for your first attempt. Start by taping some clear film or tracing paper over a large-scale map of the area to be surveyed. Using a marker pen, draw the outline of the places that you intend to visit, including obvious contours, and features such as rivers, woods and buildings. You can now transfer the outline map to a clipboard to take on your survey.

Geological maps (below) show the kinds of rocks that are under your feet, even if you cannot always see them.

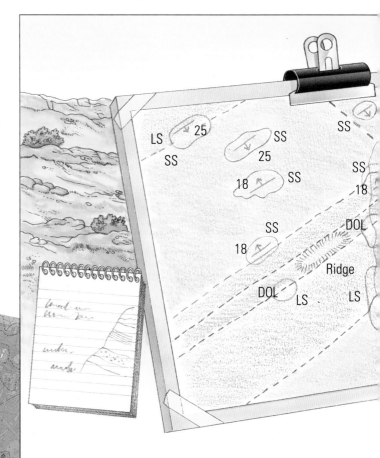

ROCKHOUND'S HINT
Never go rockhunting alone. Always tell an adult where you are going and when you will return.

THE SURVEY

To carry out your survey, plan a route that crosses the ground several times. It is best to head up and down slopes in the landscape so that you cross the layers of rock as you go. Whenever you come to a bare rock, called an outcrop, take a sample and try to identify it. Also measure the dip of the layers. Number and label samples as you go, and keep a record of your findings and measurements.

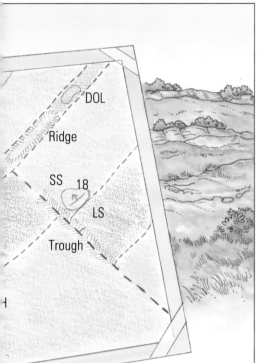

Some useful map symbols

/////	Landslip
o	Borehole, open shaft or well = DANGER!
20↑	The direction of strike, with the dip shown in degrees.
────	A line of contact between two rock layers, visible
─ ─ ─	Estimated line of a hidden contact.
— — —	Fault line
LS	Limestone
SS	Sandstone
SH	Shale
DOL	Dolerite

Making a geological survey takes a lot of time and skill, but the result is very satisfying - your own geological map.

MAKING A CLINOMETER

A clinometer is used for measuring the slope, or incline, of rock layers. To make one, cut a notch in the middle of a plastic protractor, as shown in the diagram. Glue the protractor to a piece of wood about 200mm wide, 150mm long and at least 20mm thick. Next, cut out a pointer and fix it into the notch, where the protractor lines meet. This pointer should swing freely when you tilt the block of wood. Finally, paint out the protractor numbers and renumber it as shown in the picture below.

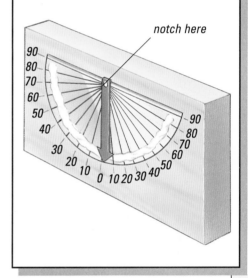

SYNCLINES AND ANTICLINES

These are two more features to include on your map. A syncline is the bottom of a fold in a section of rock, and an anticline is the top.

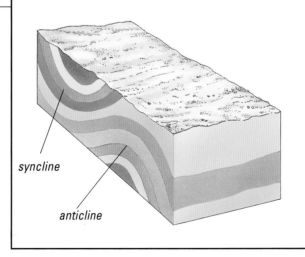

syncline

anticline

STRIKE AND DIP

Many rock layers are not horizontal. The angle at which a stratum lies is called the dip. To measure the dip of a rock, place your clinometer on the sloping layer and swing it round until you get the maximum reading. The clinometer shown here is on a dip of about 20°. Use your compass to measure the direction of the dip. The strike of the rocks is a line at right angles (90°) to the dip.

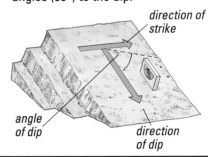

direction of strike

angle of dip

direction of dip

PROPERTIES OF MINERALS

Minerals have special properties, and you will need to know some of them before you can start to identify the samples you collect. Important properties include colour, lustre, hardness, cleavage and density, as well as the shapes of crystals and their habits (explained on page 64). Once you have worked out the properties of a sample, you can refer to the information on page 38 to help you identify it.

Goethite is usually yellow-brown or black. This unusual specimen is iridescent - it shows the colours of the rainbow.

WHY SO MANY NAMES?

Many mineral names end in the letters '-lite', from the Greek word for rock, *lithos*. The first part of the name might refer to a property of the mineral (such as the blue mineral azurite, from azure, a shade of blue), or to places where they are found (such as montmorillonite, from Montmorillon, France).

Some minerals have several names. This is because they have a number of forms, even though they are made up of the same sort of particles. For example, the mineral quartz can have several colours. It is called amethyst when purple, citrine when yellow, and smoky quartz when dark brown or black. The colours are caused by traces of impurities.

Yellow sulphur (left) is found in areas of volcanic activity.

Fluorite (above) can be a difficult mineral to identify since it is found in several colours - the green crystals here are a common form. Blue sodalite (left) is very distinctive.

THE STREAK TEST

Looking at the colour alone is not usually enough to identify a mineral. Sulphur, which is found near volcanoes, is always yellow. However, other minerals show a range of colours: feldspar crystals in granite can be white, cream or brown, for example. To find a mineral's 'true' colour, scrape it across the unglazed back of a tile. The colour of the mineral's powder mark is called the streak colour - haematite's streak (right) is red-brown. The same mineral type will produce the same streak colour on the tile even if several samples look different. This test only works for minerals that are softer than the unglazed tile. If the mineral is harder than the tile, use a steel file or nail to scratch the mineral. The powder on the scratch is the streak colour.

LUSTRE

Many minerals have surfaces that are easy to recognize. Minerals containing metals have a metallic lustre, a shiny surface that reflects light. Other minerals can have silky, glassy or even greasy lustres. When you write notes about your mineral samples, describe the surface lustre.

Pyrite has a shiny metallic lustre and forms cubic crystals.

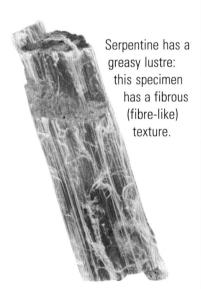

Serpentine has a greasy lustre: this specimen has a fibrous (fibre-like) texture.

Talc is the softest mineral (1 on Mohs' scale). It has a greasy lustre, and looks like soft chalk.

HARDNESS

This is one of the most useful properties of minerals to identify. The hardness scale, invented by the mineralogist Friedrich Mohs in 1822, is divided into 10 degrees of hardness. The rule is that any mineral can scratch another one of the same hardness or softer than itself. The hardest natural mineral, diamond, has a hardness value of 10 and can scratch anything else.

Using the examples of everyday objects shown in Mohs' scale, try scratching a mineral to measure its hardness. Move a sharp edge of the known object over the mineral to be tested. Now run a moistened fingertip over the surface to remove any loose powder and check that the mineral has been scratched. If you can scratch the mineral with a penknife blade but not with a copper coin, its hardness must be between 3.5 and 5.5. As your mineral collection grows, you will be able to build up a selection of the Mohs minerals for testing new finds. Mineral 10 may be a problem!

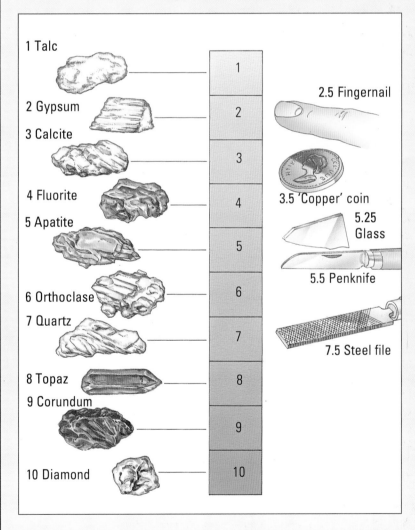

1 Talc
2 Gypsum
3 Calcite
4 Fluorite
5 Apatite
6 Orthoclase
7 Quartz
8 Topaz
9 Corundum
10 Diamond

2.5 Fingernail
3.5 'Copper' coin
5.25 Glass
5.5 Penknife
7.5 Steel file

CLEAVAGE AND FRACTURE

Some minerals and rocks can be split quite easily in particular directions. The mineral halite, a salt, is found as cubes. The cubes can be cleaved, or broken, into smaller cubes by using a hammer and sharp chisel. Many minerals will only break easily if they are hit in the right place.

Minerals and rocks will also break unevenly, or fracture. Quartz doesn't have a neat cleavage that you can see, and fractures unevenly in all directions: the fracture is called conchoidal, or shell-like. Their cleavage and fracture often helps to identify minerals and rocks.

Obsidian is rich in the mineral silica. Like quartz (see page 40), it breaks like glass with a sharp shell-like edge, called a conchoidal fracture. Calcite crystals (right) are often found with a rhombic shape. You can break them into smaller rhombs.

THE FIZZ TEST

All carbonate minerals, such as calcite, fizz when treated with a drop of weak acid such as vinegar. Wear safety glasses and protective gloves when using acid. Use a rock that you know to be a carbonate rock, such as limestone, and add a few drops of acid. Look for the fizz.

Now carefully add a few drops of acid to the sample being tested. Choose a part that contains nothing of special interest since the acid may damage the surface. Look for any evidence of fizzing. The gas being given off is carbon dioxide. Only carbonate minerals and rocks such as limestone give this test result.

ROCKHOUND'S HINT

Always wash your hands after handling minerals and carrying out tests. Also, keep your testing equipment clean so the remains of specimens tested previously don't confuse your results.

Mica (right) is well known for its cleavage into thin sheets. Some of them look like sheets of paper.

MAGNETISM

Some iron minerals are naturally magnetic. It's easy to identify them - just bring a compass near a sample, and the compass needle will point towards it.

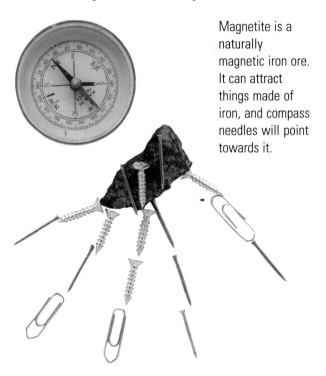

Magnetite is a naturally magnetic iron ore. It can attract things made of iron, and compass needles will point towards it.

DENSITY

Minerals that are heavier than other minerals of the same size are said to have a higher density. Most minerals have a density between 2.0 and 9.0 grams per millilitre, though some, such as gold and platinum, are as high as 19.0. Sometimes density is referred to as SG or 'specific gravity'.

The density test is a complicated one, but it does provide very useful information. First you need to weigh the mineral sample accurately in grams, say 150g. Next, measure the volume of the mineral. To do this, place some water in a measuring jug and note the volume reading. Carefully add the mineral and note the new reading. The difference between readings gives you the mineral volume, in millilitres, say 50ml. Use this formula to find the density:

$$\text{Density} = \text{mass in grams} \div \text{volume in millilitres}$$
$$= 150\text{g} \div 50\text{ml}$$
$$= 3\text{g/ml}$$

DENSITY

Find the mass in grams of the sample as accurately as you can by using scales or a balance. Kitchen scales and letter balances are quite accurate enough for large samples.

Pour some water into a measuring jug until the water level is exactly opposite one of the scale marks. Note the volume reading in millilitres.

Now add the sample you have weighed. Make sure that no water is lost by splashing. Read the new, higher, water level. The difference will give you the volume of the rock sample.

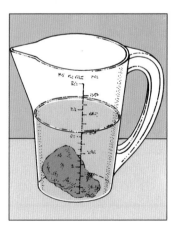

If you can't take a sample home, try to guess its weight and volume. Compare it with an object or sample for which you know or can find out the density.

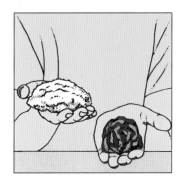

FLAME TESTS

Flame tests will show some other properties of minerals. Ask your science teacher at school to help you with flame tests. Flames and fumes can be dangerous, so be very careful.

FLAME TESTS

A gas flame is essential for carrying out some tests on rocks and minerals - school Bunsen burners are ideal for this purpose. When carrying out tests with flames and chemicals, always wear your safety glasses, and make sure that you have good ventilation. You should use pliers, or tongs and pencil leads (*not* pencils), to place the samples safely in a hot flame. Blowing air through a 15cm narrow metal or glass tube will make the flame even hotter. Have a ceramic tile ready to place hot things on safely.

FLAME COLOURS

Many minerals contain metals that give a colour to gas flames. An example of this effect is the sparkling colours of a firework display. Another is the bright orange-yellow colour given to gas flames when salty water in a saucepan boils over - this is because salt contains the metal sodium.

The flame test works best if you use small, powdered samples. Large samples on the pencil lead are difficult to clean off ready for the next test. Using pliers, clean the end of a pencil lead (*not* a pencil) by heating it in the flame. Next, dip the lead into the powdered mineral sample and return it to the flame. Make a note of the first flash of colour that you see. Different metals give characteristic flame colours that can be used to identify minerals:

Colour of the flame	Metal present in mineral
Dull red or orange	calcium
Lilac	potassium
Green-blue	copper
Bright red	strontium
Orange-yellow	sodium
Yellow sparks	iron

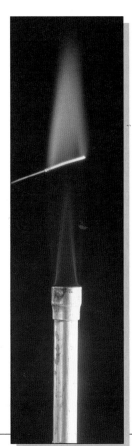

calcium *potassium* *copper* *strontium* *sodium*

BORAX BEAD TESTS

The borax bead test is another test for showing what metals are present in a mineral. It uses borax, which is a white powder that melts easily in a gas flame, to test mineral samples. You will need a clean piece of stiff wire, called nichrome wire, with a loop in the end. Borax can be obtained from a supermarket, wire from a DIY store. Crush the bead between two coins to remove it from the wire loop after the test. If the beads are black, use less powder next time.

FLAMES

In many cases the colour of the borax bead will depend on where it is heated in the gas flame. The tip of a blue gas flame is surrounded by oxygen gas in the air. This is called the 'oxidizing' flame. When there is too little oxygen for the gas to burn completely, a yellow flame is produced. Inside this 'reducing' flame, borax beads may turn different colours. The colours are shown in the table below.

Borax beads can be used to identify the metal present in a mineral sample. Different metals give different bead colours.

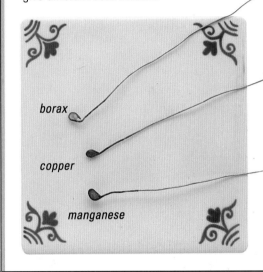

BORAX BEAD TEST

Bend the end of a strong piece of wire into a small loop around the end of a sharp pencil. Heat the loop in the flame, holding the wire in some pliers. Dip the hot loop into powdered borax.

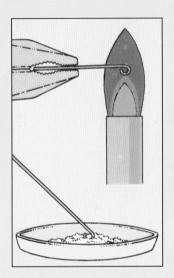

Return the borax to the flame and heat it until it swells up and then melts into a clear glassy bead.

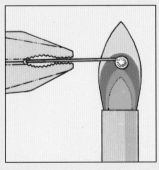

Now dip the hot borax bead on to a tiny piece of the mineral you want to test. Return it to the flame. Some minerals dissolve in the borax to give beautiful, coloured glassy beads.

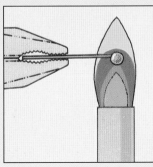

Oxidizing (blue) flame colour		Reducing (yellow) flame colour		Metal present
Hot	Cold	Hot	Cold	
yellow	green	green	green	chromium
green	blue	colourless to green	opaque red-brown	copper
yellow to orange	green to brown	bottle green	paler bottle green	iron
violet	red-brown	opaque grey	opaque grey	nickel
violet	red-violet	colourless	colourless	manganese

MINERAL DATA

The information on these pages will help you to identify some of the minerals you have collected. There are in fact over 2,500 minerals on Earth, but most of them are very rare, and the average collector is likely to find only about 300 of the most common and widespread. If you cannot find your mineral here, you will need to look in a field guide.

MINERAL DATA

Mineral	Density	Hardness	Flame	Acid	Streak
Halite	2.5	2.5	yellow	no	no
Calcite	2.7	3.0	orange	yes	white
Gypsum	2.3	2.0	orange	no	white
Fluorite	3.2	4.0	orange	no	varies
Malachite	4.0	3.5	blue	yes	green
Quartz	2.6	7.0	no	no	white
Magnetite*	5.2	6.0	no	no	black
Galena	7.5	2.5	no	no	grey
Pyrite*	5.0	6.2	no	no	green/grey
Haematite*	5.0	varies	no	no	red

Note: All the minerals marked * are minerals containing iron, but only magnetite will affect a compass needle.

SPECIAL MINERAL PROPERTIES

Some minerals have unusual or special properties. For example, one variety of the mineral calcite, calcium carbonate, is called Iceland spar. The colourless crystals have the special property of making everything appear twice. If you place an Iceland spar crystal on some writing the words can be seen twice, an effect called double refraction. The effect is even more interesting if you rotate the crystal.

FLUORESCENCE

If you have a sample of fluorite you may find that it glows in ultraviolet (UV) light. Ultraviolet lights are used on sunbeds to give a suntan, and in discos to make colours glow in the dark. You may also have seen security inks that are invisible except when placed in UV light. Minerals such as fluorite that glow like this are said to be fluorescent.

Willemite (above) is a mineral that fluoresces in ultraviolet light. Light passing through a crystal of Iceland spar (below) is split into two so that you see a double image.

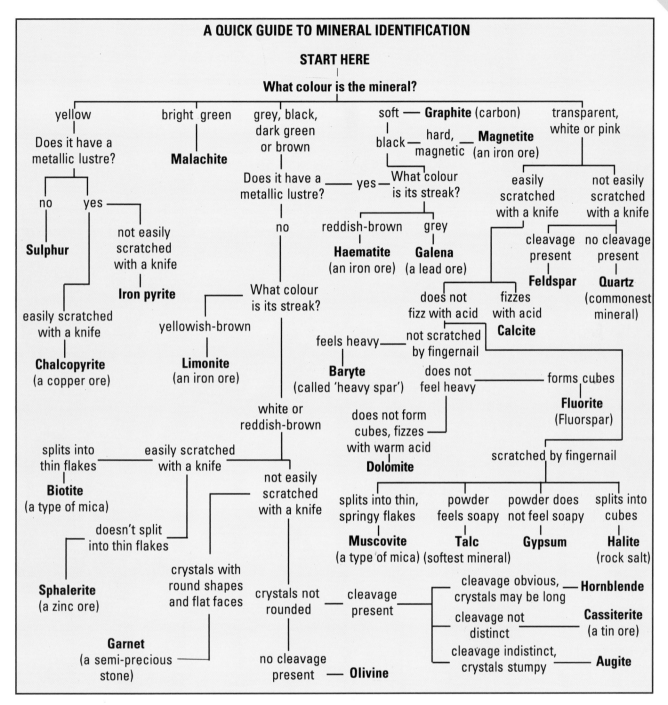

A QUICK GUIDE TO MINERAL IDENTIFICATION

START HERE

What colour is the mineral?

- **yellow** — Does it have a metallic lustre?
  - no → **Sulphur**
  - yes → not easily scratched with a knife → **Iron pyrite**
  - easily scratched with a knife → **Chalcopyrite** (a copper ore)

- **bright green** — **Malachite**

- **grey, black, dark green or brown** — Does it have a metallic lustre?
  - yes → What colour is its streak?
    - reddish-brown → **Haematite** (an iron ore)
    - grey → **Galena** (a lead ore)
  - no → What colour is its streak?
    - yellowish-brown → **Limonite** (an iron ore)
    - white or reddish-brown
      - easily scratched with a knife
        - splits into thin flakes → **Biotite** (a type of mica)
        - doesn't split into thin flakes → **Sphalerite** (a zinc ore)
      - not easily scratched with a knife
        - crystals with round shapes and flat faces → **Garnet** (a semi-precious stone)
        - crystals not rounded
          - cleavage present
            - cleavage obvious, crystals may be long → **Hornblende**
            - cleavage not distinct → **Cassiterite** (a tin ore)
            - cleavage indistinct, crystals stumpy → **Augite**
          - no cleavage present → **Olivine**

- **soft** — **Graphite** (carbon)
- **black** — hard, magnetic → **Magnetite** (an iron ore)
  - feels heavy → **Baryte** (called 'heavy spar')
  - does not feel heavy
    - does not form cubes, fizzes with warm acid → **Dolomite**
      - splits into thin, springy flakes → **Muscovite** (a type of mica)
      - powder feels soapy → **Talc** (softest mineral)
      - powder does not feel soapy → **Gypsum**
      - splits into cubes → **Halite** (rock salt)
    - forms cubes → **Fluorite** (Fluorspar)
    - not scratched by fingernail
      - does not fizz with acid
      - fizzes with acid → **Calcite**
    - scratched by fingernail

- **transparent, white or pink**
  - easily scratched with a knife
    - cleavage present → **Feldspar**
    - no cleavage present → **Quartz** (commonest mineral)
  - not easily scratched with a knife

RADIOACTIVITY

A few minerals are radioactive, that is they give off streams of invisible particles. The special meter that can detect radioactivity is called a Geiger counter. The fuel for nuclear power stations comes from radioactive minerals.

Geiger counters make a clicking sound when they detect radiation from minerals such as pitchblende.

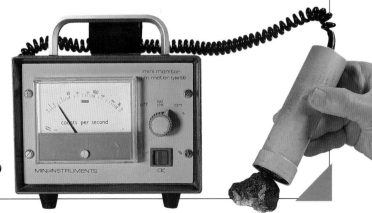

SILICA

CRYSTALLINE SILICA

The most famous varieties of silica are the quartzes used as gemstones in jewellery (see page 69). Colourless quartz is also known as rock crystal, purple quartz is amethyst and the yellow variety is citrine. All of these minerals, as well as other silica varieties such as jasper, flint and chert, can be found as pebbles on stony beaches. Many pebbles look rather disappointing since they have a white beach coating. When they are cracked open or polished the full beauty of the minerals can be seen. If you test the hardness of silica pebbles, they will be harder than a penknife blade.

The two commonest elements in the Earth's crust are silicon and oxygen. Combined, they give the commonest mineral, silica. When you go on holiday to the seaside you usually walk on powdered silica: most people call it sand. A very resistant mineral, sand is all that is left of some types of rocks that have been broken up by weathering.

A SURPRISING VARIETY

Take some small plastic bags and seals with you on holiday and start a sand collection. It is not until you have several samples from different beaches or sand dunes that you will realize how varied sand can be. The colour, size and shapes of sand grains all give evidence about the original rocks. In some places you will be able to collect many varieties of sand: a famous location is Alum Bay in the Isle of Wight.

Collecting sand samples from the beach or cliff is very easy. You will be surprised at the variety of colours and grain sizes that you can find. Some sands are found in coloured bands, so you might find several samples in one place.

citrine

rose quartz

olivine sand

smoky quartz

amethyst

beach sand

desert sand

volcanic sand

a quartz geode

A SPECIAL TYPE OF SILICA

Some volcanoes produce a natural glass called obsidian. It is a rock but is very rich in silica. It is usually black and breaks with a curved surface, just like ordinary glass. If a volcano erupts violently, molten obsidian is thrown high into the air. As it cools and falls to Earth, it will form teardrop-shaped pieces, which are sometimes known as 'Apache tears'.

jasper

chert

agate

There are many varieties of silica. The colours of rose quartz and amethyst are produced by impurities in the silica. Geodes are cavities filled with crystals, and many fine amethysts have been found in geodes. Stony beaches often contain red or brown jasper pebbles. Agates are banded and look their best when polished.

FLINT TOOLS AND THE STONE AGE

Early peoples used flint to make cutting tools. You can try to repeat this early technology by shaping an arrow head or axe. If you are careful you may be able to produce your own Stone Age toolset.

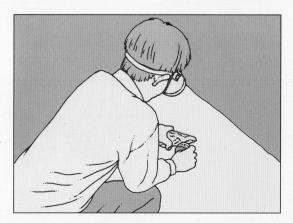

Collect some samples of flint and kneel on a thick cloth to protect your knees. Wear your safety glasses and some gloves, because flints are sharp. Hold one flint on the cloth and strike pieces off the edge using a second flint, called the flaking tool.

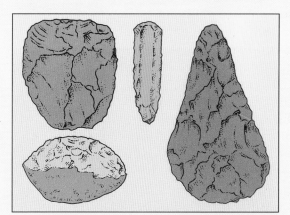

Small pieces can be chipped away to shape the flint. With some practice you will be able to produce sharp cutting edges like those made long ago. Stone Age peoples produced some very efficient flint tools and weapons, such as the hand axe, flaking tool, knife and scraper shown here.

'Apache tears'

MINERAL WATERS

Have you ever noticed that the heating elements of electric kettles become covered in white scale? This scale is calcium carbonate that had been dissolved in the water supply. You can quite easily show that the water supply contains dissolved minerals by filling a dark-coloured dish with tap water and leaving the water to evaporate. Rings of the mineral crystals will be left on the dish.

Water has eroded and dissolved the rock to form the huge limestone pinnacles pictured above. Limestone caves (below) contain incredible landscapes of lakes, rivers and columns. As water evaporates, stalactites grow from the roof as tubes.

UNDERGROUND CAVES

As rain water drains down through soil and rocks, it dissolves some of the minerals, especially the calcium carbonate of limestones. Sometimes streams dissolve a path through the rock. Gradually, large cave systems are formed underground.

The evaporation of the water inside the caves causes mineral crystals to form on the roof and floor. These stalactites and stalagmites grow very slowly, perhaps just a few millimetres each century. The surfaces of the rock in the caves also becomes covered in dripstone (calcium carbonate again).

ROCKHOUND'S HINT
Never try to explore caves and potholes. They are very dangerous. If you want to see some limestone caves, go on a properly organized guided tour.

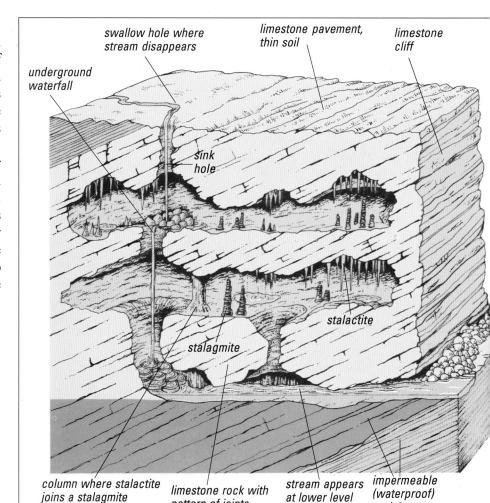

swallow hole where stream disappears

limestone pavement, thin soil

limestone cliff

underground waterfall

sink hole

stalactite

stalagmite

column where stalactite joins a stalagmite

limestone rock with pattern of joints

stream appears at lower level

impermeable (waterproof) rock layer

BOTTLED MINERAL WATERS

Many people like the taste of mineral waters and think that the dissolved materials may be good for their health. Look at the labels of some mineral water bottles, many of which give a list of the minerals that are dissolved in the water. Remember that most tap waters also contain minerals.

In some towns, there are health resorts where people can sample the mineral waters. Some of these spa towns have hot springs and all sorts of claims are made about the benefits to people's health. Some natural springs produce radioactive waters, especially in volcanic areas. Travel guidebooks will help you locate some examples of spa towns.

When water dripping from above hits a cave floor, some of it evaporates and stalagmites grow upwards. When stalactites growing from the ceiling meet stalagmites, columns form.

TASTING SAMPLES

Get together with some friends and test some different water samples for taste. You could use tap water, different bottled waters and distilled water, the purest form of all. Taste each sample then, wearing a blindfold, see if you can correctly identify them again. Next, put the samples in order of taste, starting with the one you like most. Test the water samples for hardness, which means that it has a lot of calcium carbonate dissolved in it. A hard water will not easily form bubbles when shaken with soap flakes. Using each sample in turn, see how much soap is needed to form a layer of bubbles that lasts for one minute.

WATER HARDNESS

Assemble some water samples in containers such as test tubes, together with some soap flakes and a pair of tweezers. Using the tweezers, add some soap flakes to the first water sample. Count and make a note of the number of flakes that you add.

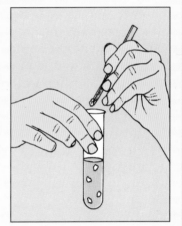

Seal the tube and shake vigorously. Stop and see if the bubbles on the surface last for at least one minute. If not, add more flakes and shake again. The harder the water sample, the more soap will be needed before the bubbles will last for one minute. Which water sample is the hardest?

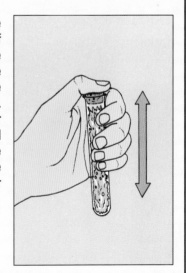

METALS FROM THE ROCKS

Most metals are found as ore minerals, where the metal is combined with other materials. To use the metal, it has to be separated, or extracted, from the waste materials. Early peoples learned how to extract metals such as copper and tin from the ores using a process of heating called smelting. They heated the ore with charcoal, to release the metal.

They soon discovered that if they smelted a mixture of copper and tin ores they could make bronze. Because it is a mixture, or alloy, of copper and tin, bronze is much stronger than either of them. Thousands of years ago, when people did not know how to smelt iron to make tools, bronze was used for jewellery, armour and cutting blades. It was so important to the civilizations that used it that it has given its name to a period of history, the Bronze Age.

THE POWER TO SUCCEED

The very earliest miners probably used sharpened deer antlers as simple picks to extract minerals from rocks. Next came the use of flint axes and, later still, bronze cutting tools. It must have been a very hard life for the early miners. In some parts of the world people are still mining by hand, just relying on muscle power.

WATER POWER

Once the miners had brought the ore from the ground, it had to be separated from the gangue minerals, the waste materials. This was called dressing the ore. Originally the ore was broken up using hammers so that the valuable ore could be collected. Once water-powered hammers had been invented, tonnes of ore could be dressed in a day.

A big problem for miners was ground water leaking into the mine and flooding it. Early miners could only use buckets to try to keep their working area dry. The invention of steam engines (below) to pump water from deep underground allowed miners to work much deeper than before.

Bronze has been used for centuries to make tools and ornaments. Shown here are a Mycenean (Greek) dagger decorated with a scene of a lion hunt (made about 1300 BC), and a head sculpted in Nigeria (from about AD 1600).

44

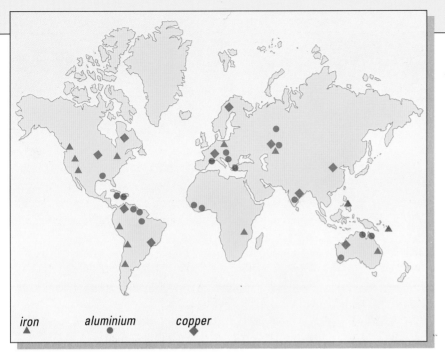

iron ▲ aluminium ● copper ◆

The map above shows some of the main areas where the important metals iron, copper and aluminium are mined commercially.

Modern trains of mineral wagons are hauled by powerful locomotives built specially to cope with the immensely heavy loads.

TAKING IT AWAY

Many mines were in remote places where there were no good roads. The miners needed to bring in supplies and take out the dressed ore ready for sale. In the early days of mining the best way to move heavy minerals was by boat, along the coast or rivers. In some areas, whole systems of canals were dug so that the valuable ores could be transported from the mines.

You can follow the development of new mines and the canals that served them by examining old maps. In some cases the mines were close to the sea so that simple mineral railways could carry the ore to the harbour. The ore wagons of the first mineral railways were dragged by horses, or even by men. However, once steam engines became small enough to be mobile, the ore wagons could be pulled by railway engines.

INDUSTRIAL ARCHAEOLOGY

In many countries it is quite easy to spot disused mine sites with their distinctive engine houses, often built of the local granite rock. Nearby will be the dumps of waste material left by the miners.

ROCKHOUND'S HINT
When you go on holiday always look out for evidence of old mineral workings, canals and railways. It will show you that you are in an area where interesting minerals can be found.

THE MOST IMPORTANT METAL

It is no accident that the Iron Age, when iron came to be used widely for tools, followed the Bronze Age. Although iron is the second most common metal in the Earth's crust, it needs a temperature of over 1,500°C for smelting. To get fires this hot, early metalworkers used charcoal to heat their furnaces. Whole forests were cut down to provide the charcoal.

The first iron bridge is still standing and is part of a museum of industrial heritage. It was so famous that the place is now called Ironbridge.

MODERN METHODS

In 1711 it was discovered that coke, made from coal, could be used instead of charcoal. This enabled the iron industry to develop new techniques for making items such as pots and pans. Soon, iron was being used for making bridges and railways, and the Industrial Revolution had begun

IRON ORES

You can find traces of iron minerals almost everywhere. When iron rusts, it combines with oxygen from the air to produce iron oxide, which is brown. This is the colour to look out for when collecting iron minerals. Most beach sands contain traces of iron oxide, and so have a brown colour. Pure sand looks like granulated sugar and is colourless.

Magnetite is the easiest iron ore to identify since it is naturally magnetic. A piece of magnetite will attract the needle of a compass. Magnetite is also called lodestone since a piece of the ore will act as a simple compass if suspended from a thread. The ore is generally black with a metallic lustre.

Another ore of iron is haematite, which can be red or black. This is one case where the streak test for minerals is invaluable. Different coloured samples of haematite all give a similar streak colour, red-brown, on a tile.

yellow limonite

brown limonite

The brown and yellow earthy forms of limonite (above) are known as ochres, and they are used to make paint. Sienna and umber, which contain aluminium, iron and manganese, are also pigments.

WEATHERING

New iron minerals form as a result of weathering (the effects of the weather). One example is limonite, which has been used for thousands of years as a pigment, a colouring. Early artists used earth that had been coloured by limonite and other mineral deposits to provide a range of colours, mostly yellows, browns, reds and black. The colour of limonite depends on the size of the mineral grains, and so many different shades can be produced.

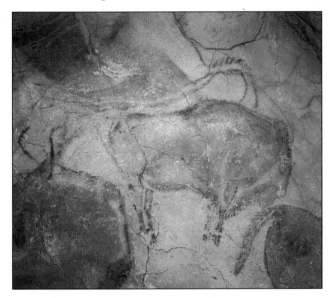

Prehistoric people made paints by mixing earth pigments and vegetables with water or animal fat. Some caves, such as those at Altamira in Spain (above), have walls that were painted more than 15,000 years ago. Colours such as blue came from minerals like azurite (below), which contains copper.

azurite

IRON FROM OUTER SPACE

Meteorites are pieces of material from outer space that have been captured by the Earth's gravity. Most meteors burn up as they fall through the atmosphere but some larger ones reach the surface. Occasionally very large meteors land, and huge craters are formed. Many meteorites are made of the metals iron and nickel. Geologists like to find meteorites because they help them understand what other stars and planets are made from.

There are some stony meteorites, but most are made of iron and nickel. You will need to be very lucky to find a meteorite, but you might see one falling through the night sky.

FOOL'S GOLD

Iron pyrite is a beautiful golden yellow mineral that many collectors have mistaken for gold. The name pyrite comes from the Greek words *pyrites lithos*, which mean 'stone which strikes fire' - pyrite will sometimes spark when struck on a lump of iron.

Iron pyrite, or 'fool's gold' (right), looks like gold and forms some wonderful crystals, but it will not make your fortune.

EXTRACT YOUR OWN METALS

Most metals are found combined with other materials. For example, tin combines with oxygen to form cassiterite. For us to be able to use them, these metals must be extracted from their naturally-occurring minerals, or ores. A few metals, such as gold and copper, are found in a pure form. They are called native metals.

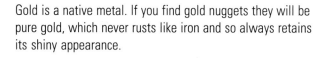

Gold is a native metal. If you find gold nuggets they will be pure gold, which never rusts like iron and so always retains its shiny appearance.

GOLD FEVER

Nobody knows how gold was first discovered, but it seems likely that gold nuggets were found first in the bed of a stream. This is because minerals are sometimes washed out of rocks as rivers flow over them. Since gold is very dense, it collects in hollows in the stream bed. In the 19th century, gold prospectors separated gold dust from sand and gravel by panning, swirling dirt and water in a pan. Try taking a pan with you when you go on holiday to the seaside. Sometimes dense minerals are washed on to a beach by streams and can be found by panning. It is also worth digging a hole in the sand and trying the panning technique on material from a lower level. You may even strike gold!

HOW TO GO PANNING

To go panning, you will need a shallow circular dish or old frying pan without the handle. Add a mixture of sand and something dense (heavy) to represent the gold, such as lead shot or iron filings. Pour in some water and swirl the mixture around. Before the water has stopped swirling, pour most of the mixture away. Any dense material should be left at the base of the pan. You can pick up magnetic metals with a magnet.

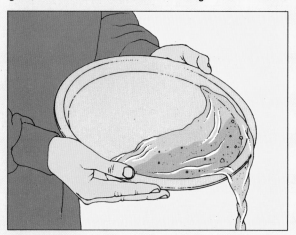

LEACHING ORES

When traces of minerals are dissolved from a rock by a liquid, it is called leaching. You will need to find a metallic ore to see how this happens: the easiest ones to use are iron or copper minerals, both of which are common.

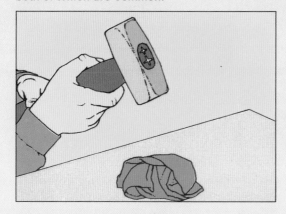

Break up about 100g of mineral by wrapping it in a cloth and hitting it with a hammer. Put the broken mineral into a filter funnel (containing filter paper) and support the funnel in the mouth of a clear jar or bottle.

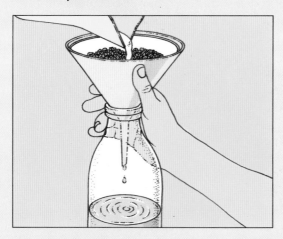

Add some strong vinegar, the leaching solution. As the liquid drains through the mineral, some of the metallic material will dissolve. The liquid that drains through, the leachate, will be blue-green if copper is present and yellow-brown for iron. You may need to pour the same liquid through more than once for the leaching to be successful.

In industry large amounts of material must be treated to remove the mineral from the waste rock. For example, some copper ores contain less than one per cent copper, the other 99 parts in 100 being waste. A simple method is needed to concentrate the valuable part of the ore. The discovery of froth flotation (above) has solved the problem.

FROTH FLOTATION

The process of froth flotation is used to concentrate valuable minerals. To see how it is done, mix some powder from sharpening a pencil (to represent the mineral) with some sand and water. Add a *little* disinfectant liquid and blow *gently* through a straw into the mixture. Do *not* drink the mixture. You will find that the mineral grains stick to the bubbles and rise to the surface of the mixture.

FOSSILS: AN AMAZING VARIETY

Everyone has seen pictures of dinosaur fossils and probably reconstructions as well. In some cases scientists have only a few bones from which to deduce what the creature looked like. You are unlikely to find dinosaur bones, but there are many other types of fossil just waiting for the collector.

AMMONITES AND BELEMNITES

Ammonites and belemnites are common as fossils. Both had hard parts that preserved easily. The soft parts of creatures - the tentacles, for example - usually leave no traces in the rocks.

Ammonites are found as shells and as impressions in rocks. The impressions left in soft sediments that eventually hardened into rock are called trace fossils. Most ammonites have curved shells, often with distinctive patterns on them. When perfect specimens are sliced in half you can see a series of chambers inside. Belemnite fossils are all that remain of creatures similar to a modern cuttlefish. Belemnites look rather like rifle bullets.

Fossils such as *micraster* (below), a form of sea urchin, are often found in chalk. They are shaped in a five-fold pattern like starfish. Sand dollars (below right) are related to sea urchins, too.

Amber can preserve creatures for millions of years, in perfect detail. The wasp on the left was caught with its prey, a fly, over 30 million years ago. Deeply-coloured amber will polish well, and is valued as a gem.

AMBER

Pine trees produce a sticky resin, and insects often become trapped in it. When this resin hardens it can become preserved as a fossil known as amber. Some specimens of amber contain insects from millions of years ago, perfectly preserved.

Bullet-shaped belemnites (right) and curly ammonites (bottom right) are found in many varieties.

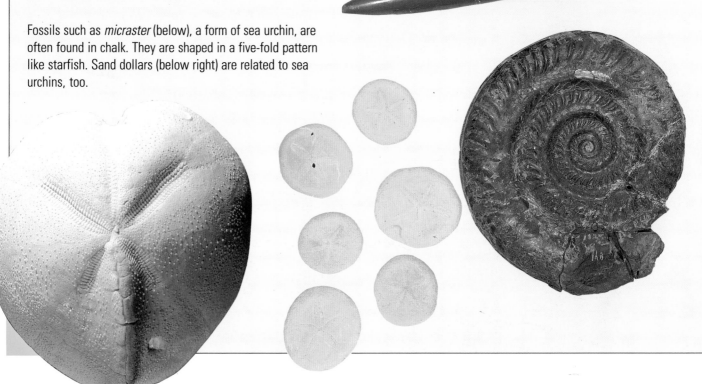

SEA URCHINS AND SEA LILIES

In chalk rock you can often find fossilized sea urchins. Usually the spines have been lost, although today's sea urchins show how the creatures might have looked millions of years ago. Sea lilies, or crinoids, are also common as fossils. The top part, or calyx, was supported on a long stem fixed to the sea bed. It is possible to find 'crinoidal' limestones where the rock is studded with pieces of broken crinoid stem. They look like little flat beads made of stone.

TRILOBITES

Among the earliest fossils to be found are the trilobites. They looked like giant woodlice but were sea creatures, scuttling about on the sea bed. Sometimes you can find their tracks in the rock, as trace fossils.

Fossil coral (left) is formed from the hard parts of ancient corals.

The descendants of the fossil sea urchins (right) still live in the sea today. Often the fossils have lost their spines.

There are many species of trilobites (above and below) to find.

Crinoids (left) must have been very common since some limestones are made almost completely of their remains.

Fossil fish and shark teeth (right) are sometimes found in large numbers. They are hard, and so preserved well as fossils when the rest of the body disappeared.

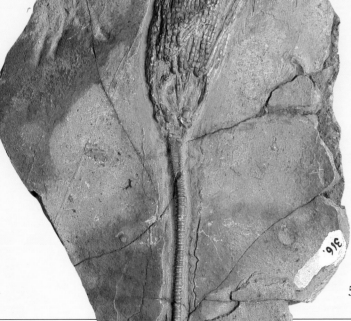

51

CASTS AND MOULDS

Sometimes the remains of a creature become covered in sediment. As the sediment slowly hardens into rock the remains may rot away completely. This leaves a hole in the rock of the same shape as the creature. This is called a mould. The people buried in the Roman city of Pompeii by the volcanic eruption of AD 79 left moulds.

When plaster of Paris is poured into a mould, the original shape can be seen. The plaster forms a cast of the fossil. This process also happens naturally when minerals dissolved in ground water collect in a fossil mould. When the rock is broken open there is a cast inside, perhaps made of calcite or quartz. None of the original material remains.

TRACKS

There are many examples of tracks left by creatures long ago. Fossilized footprints from both dinosaurs and people have been found in rocks. In fact, some dinosaurs are known only from their tracks: no bones have been found yet.

Just like footprints in the sand, dinosaurs left tracks (above) that are sometimes preserved in hard rock.

Splitting a block of limestone revealed this ammonite (above). The shell along the outer spiral has split away. Inside, calcite crystals have grown into the space where the ammonite's fleshy body lived. Often a fossil is partly covered by rock (left). With great care the covering can be scraped or dissolved away to show the full detail (see page 15).

Most wood rots after trees have died, but sometimes the wood is replaced by minerals and an amazing fossil forest is formed (right).

FOSSIL CASTS

 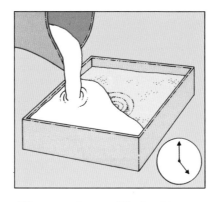 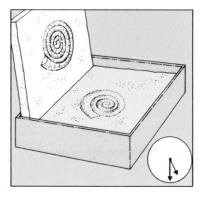

Place a 2cm deep layer of damp sand in a shallow tray to represent a soft sediment. Press a fossil, seashell or other small object into the sand to make a clear impression.

Mix some plaster of Paris with water to form a smooth paste, and pour it over the sand, making sure that the impression is completely covered. Wait until the plaster has set hard.

Carefully lift the plaster and examine the cast of the impression in the sand. Many fossils are preserved like this.

PETRIFIED WOOD

Coal is one example of fossilized plants, but there are some others. When forests became covered by water or fallen trees became waterlogged, the wood is sometimes preserved intact. However, silica in ground waters can replace the woody material, leaving a quartz fossil. Some of this fossilized wood is harder than steel, and the tree rings can still be counted. Museums display polished slices of fossilized wood.

LEAF CASTS

You can also make casts of leaf fossils using plasticine as a base. First, make a bed with the plasticine, then cover it with petroleum jelly to prevent the plasticine and plaster of Paris sticking together. Press a ribbed leaf into the plasticine to make an impression.

Remove the leaf and build up some plasticine walls, smeared with petrol jelly, to hold in the plaster. Pour in the mixed plaster and leave it to set.

HOW OLD ARE THEY?

The serious study of fossils did not start until the 19th century. Although fossils had been known for centuries, they were not originally recognized as being the remains of living things. Even in the 19th century, some naturalists claimed that it was simply a coincidence that fossils looked like some living creatures or plants.

A SERIOUS SUBJECT

One of the first geologists to take fossils seriously was Frenchman Georges Cuvier. His studies in the early 19th century resulted in palaeontology - the study of past living things - being recognized as a separate science. It was Cuvier who identified and named the flying creature pterodactyl.

THE USE OF SCIENCE

Today the study of fossils is aided greatly by technology. There are ways in which the ages of rocks and fossils can be calculated, by measuring traces of radioactive material in them. Once the age of a fossil is known, it can be used to date other rocks that contain the same type of fossil. Fossilized creatures also provide evidence about the environment and climate of the time they were alive.

This table divides up the Earth's history into smaller parts, each with its own name and age of millions of years. The details of the table are constantly being changed as scientists learn more.

THE STRATIGRAPHICAL TABLE

Even though modern technology can help them with their studies, geologists have to make certain assumptions about the ages of rocks and fossils. One is known as the Law of Superposition. It says that when examining strata, younger rocks will be above older ones, since they formed more recently.

Using the study of strata, scientists have divided the Earth's history up into periods of time. The information is contained in a diagram called the stratigraphical table (below). This geological time-scale took many years to develop. Studies of rock strata from one area can be used to date rocks, and the fossils they contain, in other areas.

ERA	PERIOD		EPOCH		millions of years ago
Cenozoic	Quaternary				2 / 5
	Tertiary	Neogene	Holocene / Pleistocene	Pliocene / Miocene	25
			Oligocene		38
		Paleogene	Eocene		55
			Paleocene		65
Mesozoic	Cretaceous				146
	Jurassic				208
	Triassic				245
Palaeozoic	Permian				290
	Carboniferous	Pennsylvanian			
		Mississippian			363
	Devonian				409
	Silurian				439
	Ordovician				510
	Cambrian				570
	Precambrian				610

HOW OLD ARE THEY?

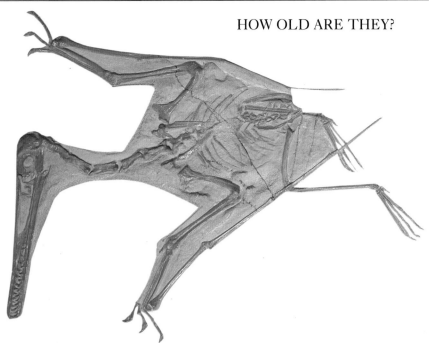

The pterodactyl or pterosaur (don't pronounce the 'p') was a flying reptile and is very rare as a fossil. Study of the fossil on the left shows the light bones and traces of wing material stretched over them. Pterodactyls may have rested like modern bats, upside down on tree branches or rocks. Some features are similar to modern birds. Pterodactyl fossils are of the Jurassic and Cretaceous Age, about 100-200 million years old.

THE FIRST FOSSILS

Scientists believe that the Earth is about 4,600 million years old. The earliest traces of fossil life in the rocks are much more recent than this, however, because only some things are likely to be preserved as fossils. Shells and bones are hard and so are often found as fossils, but the early creatures were like soft worms and jellyfish and so have not often been preserved. Nevertheless, there is evidence for simple creatures like algae nearly 2,000 million years ago.

As we come closer to the present, more complicated living things begin to appear in the fossil record. Almost all the common fossils that you will find date from the last 600 million years.

A GIANT JIGSAW

Sometimes fossils of land creatures of the same species and age are found on both sides of an ocean. How did they get there? One explanation is that all the land on the Earth was originally joined together. A theory called plate tectonics suggests that land masses drift slowly across the Earth's surface. Over millions of years they have travelled great distances. Thus continents that are now separated by water could once have been joined together.

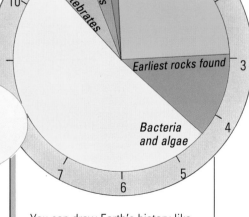

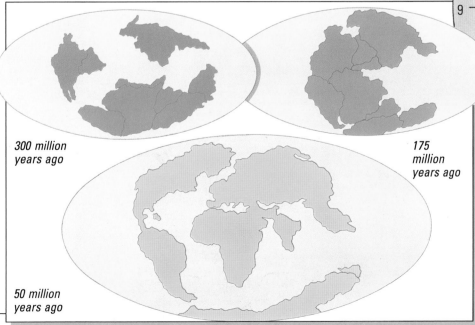

300 million years ago

175 million years ago

50 million years ago

You can draw Earth's history like a clock face (above). It shows in which order life appeared on the planet. There is good evidence that the shapes and positions of the land masses (left) have changed greatly over that time.

MAKING YOUR NAME

Fossil hunting can be great fun and the finders may even make history. One fossil hunter who became famous was an English schoolgirl from Lyme Regis in Dorset. Mary Anning was only 11 years old when she discovered the first fossil *Ichthyosaurus*, a large sea-living creature, in 1810. She went on to make many more fossil discoveries and is commemorated in a church stained glass window.

THE FINDER'S NAME
Some people who find new types of creature are lucky enough to have the creature named after them. For example, the dinosaur *Protoceratops andrewsi* ('Andrews' early horned head') was named after Roy Chapman Andrews. He was the leader of an American expedition that found over 100 *Protoceratops* skeletons in Mongolia in the early 1920s. Many other dinosaurs are named after their finders.

Mary Anning (left) was one of the pioneers of fossil collecting. She discovered bones of an *Icthyosaurus* (below), a huge aquatic reptile from about 200 million years ago. If you find a new type of fossil, you, too, could become famous.

The coelacanth has been a very successful survivor. It is known to have existed for millions of years.

Careful study of the fossils of *Baryonyx walkeri* (Walker's Big Claw) has led to a reconstruction (left) to show how the creature might have looked. It was named in part after its finder, amateur collector William Walker.

LIVING FOSSILS

There are some creatures described as living fossils. These are ones that are known from the fossil record but were thought to be extinct. One of the most famous is a fish called a coelacanth. Fossils of coelacanths have been found in rocks as old as 400 million years and as young as 65 million years. After this, there was no evidence of the coelacanth surviving until a living specimen was caught by fishermen off the coast of Madagascar in 1938. Since then other specimens of this living fossil have been found.

CAREFUL RESEARCH

When you start a fossil collection of your own, find out as much as possible about them from local museums and books. Once you become familiar with the range of fossils in a particular area you will know when something unusual turns up. Some people have made a living as fossil collectors.

A knowledge of the main rock types will be a great help when you are collecting. Don't forget, there is little point in searching for fossils in igneous rocks such as granite since there are none. It is the main types of sedimentary rock that will provide you with fossils for your collection.

There are many ways in which bones can be joined together to form a skeleton, especially if some of the bones are missing. This is a reconstruction of *Triceratops*, 'three-horned head', whose massive bone skull preserves well as a fossil.

FOSSILS AND OIL

The world's first oil well was drilled in the USA in 1859. This was the start of the world's biggest industry, the oil industry. Oil is used to generate the electricity used in homes and industry, and to power our transport. It is also used to make most of our plastics, rubbers and synthetic fibres ('man made' materials such as nylon).

OIL EXPLORATION

In some parts of the world, oil and natural gas escape naturally at the surface of the ground. In the Middle East there are 'eternal fires', places where escaping gas has been burning naturally for thousands of years. On some seashores oil seeps out naturally from the rocks. Obviously, signs like this give geologists strong indications that more oil and natural gas are buried underground. Some of the deposits of oil are under the sea bed, such as those in the North Sea. Many more, such as the huge Texan and Middle Eastern oilfields, are under dry land.

Drilling oil wells is very expensive, often costing many millions of pounds for a single well. Therefore geologists need as much evidence as possible of the presence of large quantities of oil before starting to drill. If oil is suspected, rock samples are collected and examined, and surveys of the whole area are carried out. If the prospects for finding oil look good, holes are drilled to examine the rocks underground.

Oil and natural gas, such as methane, are usually found together. Sometimes waste gas must be 'flared off' (above) before the oil can be transported safely for processing at oil refineries.

PROSPECTING METHODS

Before drilling an oil well, geologists must survey the rocks to see if they are of the right type and structure to contain oil. In one method (below), a small explosion is used to send shock waves down to the rock layers below. Microphones detect the

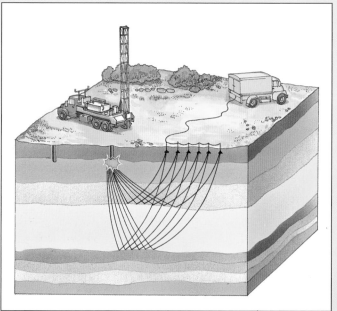

Nodding donkeys (right) are pumps that bring oil to the surface from the underground oilfield. Sometimes microfossils (below) provide evidence of oil deposits.

LOOKING FOR FOSSILS

The drills provide both rock chippings and core samples for further study. Since the samples are small it is unlikely that ordinary fossils will be present. Luckily there are other types of fossil that are of great interest to the oil geologist. These are the microfossils (very small fossils) that can be present in rock chippings in great numbers.

Extracting and studying microfossils is a job for the experts. The rock samples must be crushed to release the fossils, and microscopes are needed to examine them in detail. One type of microfossil is known as the foraminifera, which is found very widely in oil-bearing rocks. Since oil and gas can move through the rocks over long periods of time, the fossils may still be there even though the oil has escaped. Therefore finding some foraminifera in the rock does not *prove* that oil is there as well, but it provides more evidence that the area being searched is a good one.

MATCHING ROCKS

Plant spores are another type of microfossil. Geologists try to match the types of plant spores in an area where coal or oil has been found, with spores in rocks of a similar age in another area. The new area may be worth investigating for oil deposits if the microfossils in the rocks are the same.

patterns of echoes, which give information about the rock structure. Vibrosis (below) is used in built-up areas. In this method, heavy weights are dropped on the ground to set up the shock waves.

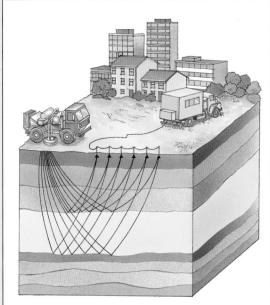

Geologists use special drills to bring up rock cores. They can then study the rock samples, such as this conglomerate.

CRYSTALS

Have you ever fractured a bone? If you have, then you've probably had an X-ray. Scientists have used X-rays in the same way to examine solids to find out about the arrangement of particles - called atoms - inside them. A crystal is a solid that is made up of atoms arranged in an orderly pattern. The edges of perfect crystals are straight, and the angles between the edges are the same size for the same kinds of crystal. The atoms inside crystals are arranged in a very regular way.

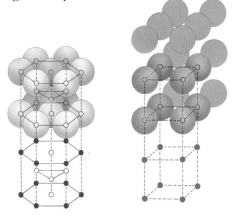

These diagrams show two ways in which particles are arranged in a regular and repeating way in a crystal. On the left is a hexagonal arrangement, on the right a cubic one.

CRYSTAL SYSTEMS

Crystals can be described according to their shapes. The shapes of crystals reflect the arrangement of atoms inside them. There are seven crystal shapes or 'systems', called cubic, tetragonal, hexagonal, orthorhombic, monoclinic, triclinic and trigonal. When identifying minerals, which are crystalline, one of the questions you will have to answer is which crystal system the mineral represents. Many samples that you collect will not have perfectly formed crystals, so you will have to make an intelligent guess!

BUBBLE RAFTS

One way of showing how atoms arrange themselves in crystals is to use a bubble raft. Make some soapy water in a shallow dish and, using a straw, blow enough bubbles to cover the surface. You will find that the bubbles form regular arrangements and patterns. Using a ruler, move rows of bubbles past each other.

CRYSTAL SYSTEMS

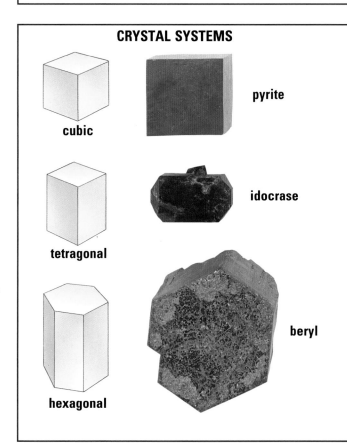

cubic

pyrite

tetragonal

idocrase

hexagonal

beryl

How easy is it? Use straws of different diameters to make bubbles of different sizes. In crystalline alloys, mixtures of metals, the 'bubbles' will be of different sizes, too. See how this makes it more difficult for the layers of bubbles to slide past each other. This is why alloys are stronger than pure metals.

CRYSTAL MODELS

You can try making some model crystals to see the ways in which the separate atoms are arranged inside. Using marbles or ball bearings, drop them a few at a time into a cardboard frame. Even though the marbles are dropped or poured in a random manner, they will line up to produce a regular pattern. The atoms will have the same angle between them. It is easiest to start with a square frame, but you can also try frames of different shapes.

Make a cardboard frame, about 10cm along each side, to hold some marbles. If you use larger objects as 'atoms', you will need to use a bigger tray, too.

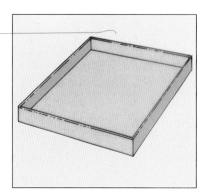

Pour a stream of marbles into the frame from just above the centre point. Collect any marbles that escape and pour them in again. Can you see a pattern forming?

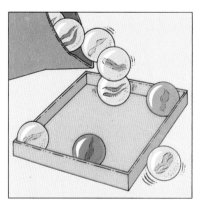

Here is one result of dropping some marbles into a square tray. If real atoms behave like this, you can see how a regular structure is built up, forming a beautiful crystal.

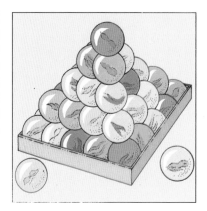

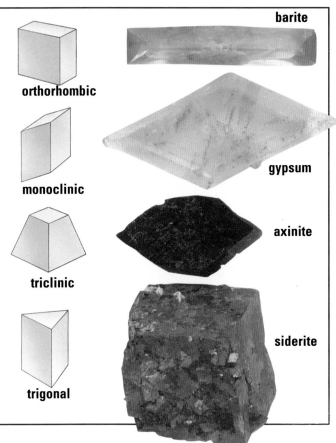

orthorhombic

monoclinic

triclinic

trigonal

barite

gypsum

axinite

siderite

GROWING CRYSTALS

It is very easy to grow crystals. Some crystals don't need much help at all. For example, crystals of calcium carbonate grow inside kettles when they are heated. Or you can leave different water samples to evaporate on saucers, and use a magnifying glass to examine the solids left behind. The home-grown crystals described on these pages can be very beautiful and grow to a large size if you are patient. Blue copper sulphate crystals always grow very well, but there are lots of others you can try. Alums come in different colours although the crystal shape is the same. You can even grow one alum crystal on top of a different coloured one.

HOME-GROWN CRYSTALS

The best crystals take a long time to grow. You can use copper sulphate for blue crystals, magnesium sulphate for colourless ones or the alums for a variety of colours. All of these chemicals are likely to be found in a chemistry set, or a pharmacist may agree to sell you some, with your parents' agreement.

The technique for growing the crystals is the same in each case. Dissolve as much of the powdered solid in hot water as you can. Stir all the time to help the solid dissolve. Filter the mixture (through coffee filter paper, for example) to take out any undissolved solid. Leave the saturated solution (a solution that is full up with the dissolved material) to cool and evaporate. After a few days crystals will form and grow.

BIGGER STILL

If you want to make some *very* large crystals, choose a well-shaped crystal from the experiment above. Tie a thread to it and suspend it in the same solution, topping it up with extra saturated solution as it evaporates. If you carry on long enough you may need a dustbin to hold the growing crystal and its solution.

You will never grow a crystal like this! It is a beautiful crystal of apatite growing on albite, a form of feldspar. Apatite is the main mineral found in bones and teeth.

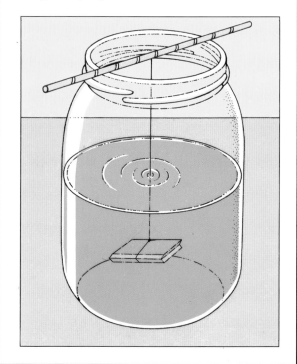

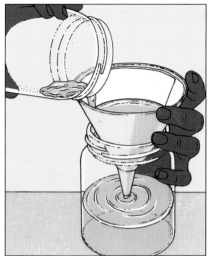

HYPO CRYSTALS

You should wear your safety glasses for this experiment. Hypo is short for sodium thiosulphate, a chemical used by photographers. Place about 12 grams of hypo crystals in a boiling tube (ask your science teacher if you can borrow one of these) and add a few drops of water. Carefully warm the mixture over a flame (below left). Warm the mixture just enough to give a clear liquid: do *not* boil it. Set aside the mixture to cool without any disturbance.

When the tube is completely cold again, add one hypo crystal as a seed crystal (below right). What happens around the edges of the seed crystal? What do you notice about the temperature?

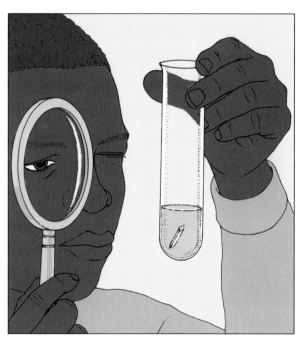

COMMERCIAL USES

Very pure crystals are grown for use in industry. Crystals are needed in lasers, and for silicon chips, the material needed to make electronic circuits for computers and calculators. Before the invention of electronic digital watches, ruby crystals were grown to make into low-friction bearings used to make mechanical watches.

Special crystals are also needed to make holograms, the pictures that seem to be in 3-D, or three dimensions. Holograms are used as security markings for bank cheque and credit cards.

CRYSTAL HABITS

Unfortunately, natural crystals often don't form as perfectly as the ones you can grow, because they don't grow in perfect conditions. Their shape can vary depending on the development of the individual faces. Also, large single crystals are comparatively rare. You are much more likely to find minerals as large groups of crystals, called aggregates.

Some of the names that scientists have given these crystal shapes are quite difficult to remember. The important thing for a collector to note is what a specimen looks like. The proper scientific description can be looked up in a book later, when you are writing up your notes. On the next page are some of the crystal habits with their scientific names.

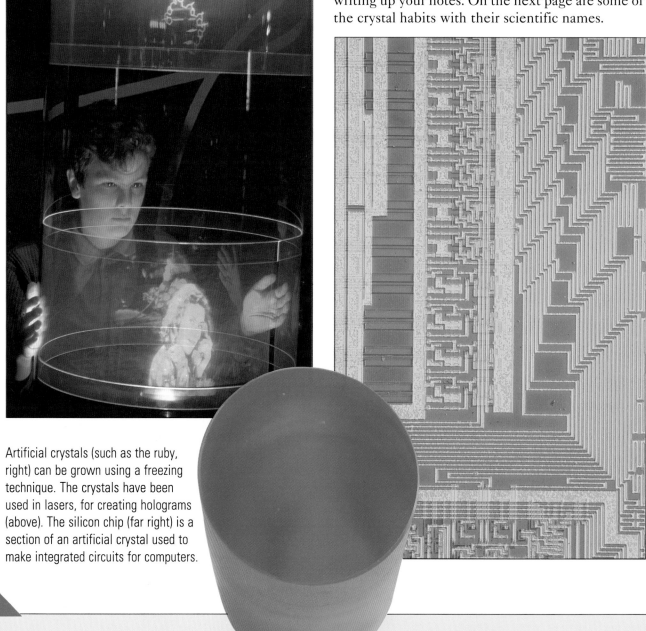

Artificial crystals (such as the ruby, right) can be grown using a freezing technique. The crystals have been used in lasers, for creating holograms (above). The silicon chip (far right) is a section of an artificial crystal used to make integrated circuits for computers.

SOME CRYSTAL HABITS

Description	Appearance	Scientific Name
sheets	sheets that can easily be split	foliated
spheres	very like round balls	globular
grapes	formed of rounded masses, like a bunch of grapes	botrvoidal
columns	like columns	columnar
hairy	like a dense mass of hair or fibre	fibrous
fern-like	looks like branches of a fern or tree	dendritic
blades	thin, narrow strips	bladed
netted	like the mesh of a net	reticulated
radiating	spreading outward from a single point	radiating
spiky	lots of needles, like a hedgehog	acicular

Pyrophyllite is a very soft glassy mineral that can be found in radiating form (shown here).

The spiky needles in the quartz (below) are crystals of rutile.

Crystals of marcasite are often shaped like spears (below).

Wolframite (below) is an ore of the metal tungsten. Wolframite crystals are long, bladed prisms.

Some crystals grow as 'twins', identical or mirror images of each other. This is a calcite 'butterfly' twin.

Actinolite (below) is a mineral that is rich in iron. It has long bladed crystals.

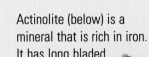

This fine specimen of native copper has an irregular branching, or dendritic, habit.

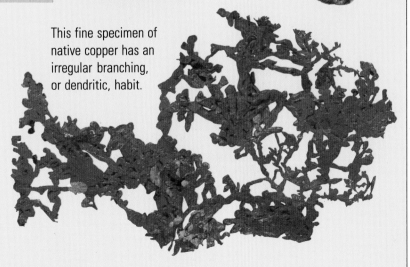

CRYSTALS AROUND US

Crystals are found not just in minerals and rocks, but all around us. In fact, virtually all naturally-occurring solids are crystalline.

CRYSTALLINE FOOD

Almost every day of your life you eat some crystals. Table salt is crystals of sodium chloride. Salt crystals are cubic in shape. You can examine some different types of salt using a hand-lens to compare the crystal shapes. Sometimes the edges become rounded during the manufacturing process.

In many parts of Europe there are the remains of Roman salt works. Salt water, called brine, was heated in large saltpans to evaporate the water and leave salt crystals behind. Where the weather was warm enough, the heat of the sun was used to evaporate seawater. This method of producing salt is still used in places such as Brittany in France, and Australia.

SWEET CRYSTALS

Another crystalline food is sugar. Sugar is not a mineral - it comes from plants, not rocks - but the particles inside it are arranged in the same way as a mineral's. See how many different sugar crystals you can find at home or at the supermarket.

Salt crystals (above) are cubic, although their size may vary. They can be extracted from brine in saltpans (below left). Although sugar is often sold as a fine powder, there are lots of crystalline varieties (below). Coloured crystals may be raw cane sugar (brown) or have had colours added to them.

SOME USES OF CRYSTALS

Metals are crystalline, although it is not always easy to see the crystal structure. One example of the use of metal crystals is called galvanizing. This is a process of putting a layer of zinc crystals onto iron items, such as nails, to stop the iron going rusty. The galvanized iron used to make wheelbarrows or buckets has large zinc crystals on its surface.

Early radio sets were called crystal wireless sets. In order to make them pick up a radio transmission, the user had to position a fine wire in exactly the right place on a crystal of galena. The wire was referred to as a cat's whisker because it was so thin, and getting the crystal set to work was quite an art.

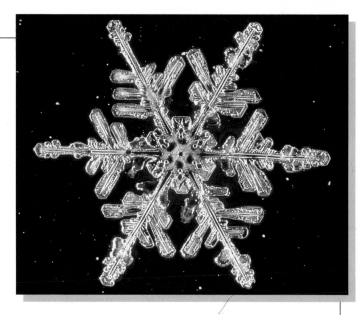

Ice crystals always form regular shapes of repeating units. It is often said that no two snowflakes are the same!

SEEDING THE SKY

During a drought, aircraft can be used to seed rainclouds with silver iodide crystals to encourage raindrops to form. This is a very expensive way to water the ground!

Did you know that crystals fall out of the sky in cold weather? Snow flakes are crystals. You can study them by collecting them on glass microscope slides that have first been cooled in a freezer. You can also grow ice crystals by putting a piece of damp cloth in a freezer: choose a dark-coloured surface so that the crystals show up clearly.

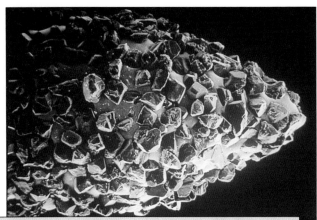

Diamonds are used to stud the tips of dentist drills (top) and for rock drills. Galena crystals were used in early crystal radio sets. Galena is one of the main ores of lead and often forms beautiful cubic crystals (above).

A HARD SURFACE

Silica (quartz) is one of the minerals found in granite. With corundum powder it can be used to make sandpaper. The hard silica and corundum crystals smooth other surfaces. Artificial crystalline materials, such as silicon carbide, can be used to make these abrasive papers, too.

Corundum is made of aluminium oxide, the same chemical that forms rubies. Corundum is useful as an abrasive.

DIAMONDS ARE FOREVER

In industry (left), diamonds are used for cutting other hard materials. Industrial diamonds can now be made artificially.

The hardest natural mineral is diamond. On the Mohs scale it has a hardness of 10. It is this property of diamond which inspired the famous advertising slogan 'diamonds are forever'. Yet diamonds are made of the common element, carbon. As long ago as 1695, scientists in Florence demonstrated that diamonds disappear when heated in air - when they burn they produce very expensive carbon dioxide gas!

Diamonds have been used in jewellery (right) for centuries, either on their own or with other gemstones.

HOT AND HARD

Diamonds are formed under conditions of high temperatures and pressures. They are mined in ancient volcanic pipes, the remains of extinct volcanoes where these conditions would have existed. By reproducing these conditions it is possible to make artificial diamonds from another form of carbon called graphite. (Graphite is the material from which pencil leads are made.) Diamonds have occasionally been found in meteorites from outer space.

DIAMONDS AT WORK

Almost all diamonds are used in industry. Since they are so hard, diamonds are used at the cutting edges of rock drills and for polishing other hard materials. In fact, only about 20 per cent of diamonds are used in jewellery. The largest diamond ever found was the Cullinan stone from South Africa. It was 3106 metric carats (a unit of weight) in size, the equivalent of about 620 grammes. It was presented to King Edward VII of Britain in 1907.

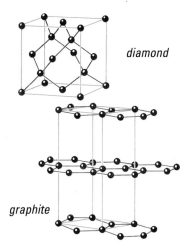

diamond

graphite

Although they are both made up of carbon atoms, graphite and diamond have very different structures. This explains why graphite is quite soft whereas diamond is so hard.

This fabulous necklace (left) is studded with over one hundred diamonds and rubies. Onyx and diamond, with emeralds for the eyes, were used to make the panther bracelet and clip (below). Each gem has been cut and polished individually before being mounted in silver.

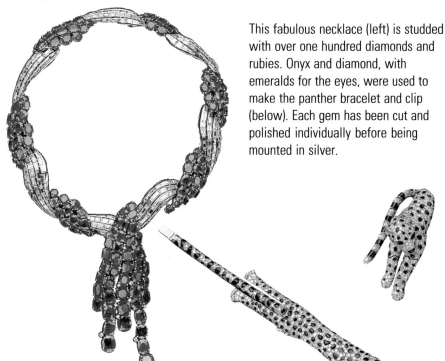

68

Uncut diamonds look very different to the cut and polished ones used in jewellery. Diamonds can be cut using other diamonds to give finished gems.

SEMI-PRECIOUS STONES

You may not find any diamonds for your collection but there are lots of other semi-precious gemstones. On many pebble beaches you might find examples of the quartz family of stones. Examples include citrine, jasper, flint, chalcedony, agate, rose quartz and smoky quartz.

TUMBLE-POLISHING

To see the full beauty of these stones they need to be polished or varnished. You can polish stones by hand using emery paper but it is slow and very hard work. The best technique to use is tumble polishing. This uses a machine that has a rotating drum into which you place the pebbles, a grinding powder and some water. It can take weeks of polishing to achieve a mirror-like polish. Once the stones are polished they can be set into holders to make your own jewellery. Tumble polishers are very noisy so you will need an isolated garage or understanding neighbours.

Most hobby shops sell beginners' polishing kits, or you could construct a tumble-polisher yourself. All you need is a screwtop plastic drum and a slow-running electric motor to turn it.

Tumble polishing can turn dull pebbles from the beach into shiny and beautiful stones.

HOW A DIAMOND IS CUT

Rough diamonds can vary a great deal in shape. They often have to be split (cleaved) before they are cut (shaped) and polished. Diamonds are cut and given faces, called facets, by holding them against a revolving metal plate covered in diamond dust - nothing else is hard enough to cut them! The huge Cullinan diamond was cut in Amsterdam into nine large stones and 96 smaller stones.

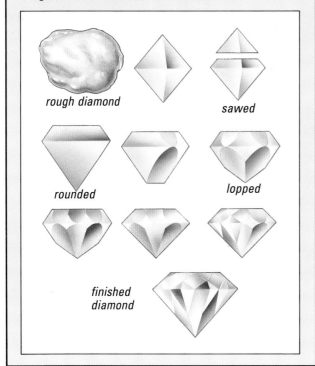

rough diamond

sawed

rounded

lopped

finished diamond

LITTLE GEMS

All gems, such as diamond and amethyst, are precious stones made of minerals. They are considered particularly valuable when cut and polished, although many people believe that good examples of the natural crystals are just as beautiful. Usually, it is the beautiful, rare and hard-wearing minerals that have had the greatest value for mounting in jewellery.

A RARE BEAUTY

Gems have been collected and used for thousands of years. Centuries ago, gems were being carved in China, and in Germany there is a tradition of carving cameos that dates back to the Romans. Cameos are produced by cutting away coloured layers of material to reveal other layers below.

During the Middle Ages, gemstones were thought to have magical healing properties, a belief that has recently come back into fashion. Jewellers set the gem so that it was in contact with the skin of the wearer. The idea was to allow what were believed to be 'health-giving rays' to enter the body.

In astrology, each month of birth has birthstones. Many people believe that wearing your birthstone brings you luck. 1: Garnet (January). 2: Amethyst (February). 3: Aquamarine (above) and bloodstone (below) (March). 4: Diamond (above) and rock crystal (below) (April). 5: Emerald and chrysoprase (May). 6: Moonstone and pearl (June). 7: Ruby and cornelian (July). 8: Peridot and sardonyx (August). 9: Lapis lazuli and sapphire (September). 10: Tourmaline and opal (October). 11: Topaz (November). 12: Zircon and turquoise (December). The sardonyx (8) is in the form of a cameo.

A QUESTION OF LUCK?

It was also believed that gems could be worn as lucky charms to gain benefits such as health and prosperity. Today, most people do not believe that gems contain magic, but still hope that they will bring good fortune to the wearer, particularly if it's the special stone for the month they were born. The wearing of these 'birthstones', such as garnet for January, is quite popular.

Some gems are associated with bad luck. The best example is opal. During the European 'Black Death' of the Middle Ages, opal was believed to shine when the wearer caught the plague and go dull when they died. Opal is also thought to be unlucky because it sometimes cracks if given a hard knock, even though it is quite a hard mineral.

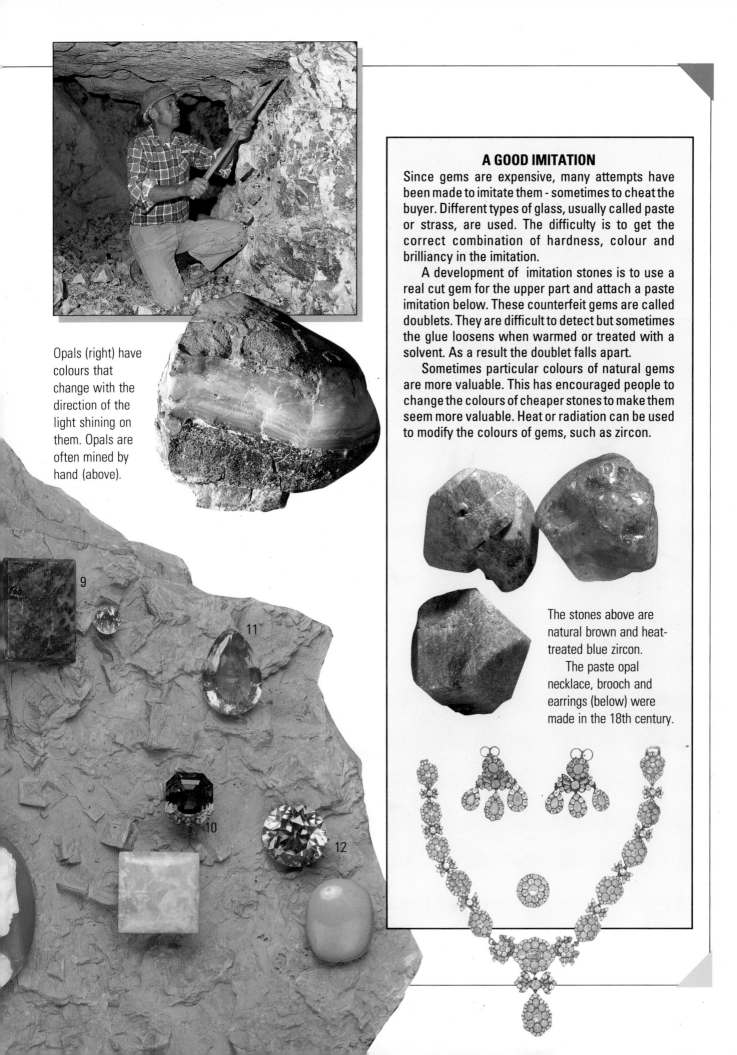

Opals (right) have colours that change with the direction of the light shining on them. Opals are often mined by hand (above).

A GOOD IMITATION

Since gems are expensive, many attempts have been made to imitate them - sometimes to cheat the buyer. Different types of glass, usually called paste or strass, are used. The difficulty is to get the correct combination of hardness, colour and brilliancy in the imitation.

A development of imitation stones is to use a real cut gem for the upper part and attach a paste imitation below. These counterfeit gems are called doublets. They are difficult to detect but sometimes the glue loosens when warmed or treated with a solvent. As a result the doublet falls apart.

Sometimes particular colours of natural gems are more valuable. This has encouraged people to change the colours of cheaper stones to make them seem more valuable. Heat or radiation can be used to modify the colours of gems, such as zircon.

The stones above are natural brown and heat-treated blue zircon.

The paste opal necklace, brooch and earrings (below) were made in the 18th century.

9

11

10

12

STORAGE AND DISPLAY

Once your collection begins to grow, you will need to plan how best to store and display your specimens. Be selective when choosing samples to take home, because rocks and fossils take up much more space than stamps, for example - you will only be able to display some of them. As your collection builds up, choose the best specimens to display, and store the others. As you replace samples with better ones, save the old ones in case they can be used in tests or swapped with other collectors - a very good way to extend the range of your own collection.

STORAGE

For basic storage of specimens you will need some trays that can be divided into compartments. Secondhand furniture may provide you with the basics: office filing cabinets or cupboards equipped with shelves would both be suitable. The cheapest method is to construct trays yourself using hardboard and strips of wood. Another advantage of home construction is that you can design trays of different sizes to fit your own specimens.

Large specimens (right) can safely be displayed on shelves. It may be better to store small, light or fragile samples in trays (below).

You can use cardboard boxes or strips of wood or card to separate your specimens in their trays. Divisions improve the look of the collection as well as organizing it.

DISPLAY

Illuminated glass shelves are a good way to display the most interesting examples from your collection. Experiment with light shining at different angles to get the best effect from your specimens. Even if you don't have space for glass shelving, why not change your display occasionally, bringing out new specimens just as they do in museums?

You can include maps of the areas you have visited as part of your display, especially geological maps that show the underlying rock strata. A collection of field sketches and line drawings of fossils or other samples will also look attractive. If you collect samples such as beach sand you may need to store and display them in different ways. For example, stoppered glass or plastic containers will be suitable for powders or other small samples.

Museum displays will give you ideas about how to show off your most prized specimens. Include a reference card with each sample so that other people can read the full details.

KEEPING RECORDS

A good system for keeping records is essential, since your collection may grow to contain hundreds of specimens. To label your samples, paint a small spot of enamel paint on to each of them. When the paint is dry, add a reference number. You can extend the system by colour coding, using white for minerals, yellow for fossils, for example.

Write the same reference number on to a file card, together with details of the sample. If you have the use of a computer with a spreadsheet, you can keep computer records instead. With a word-processing program the records can be more comprehensive and are easily updated.

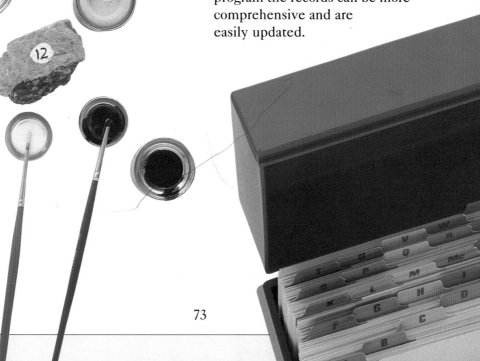

Use bright enamel paint to place reference spots and numbers on specimens. Use different colours for the different types. A simple card index will make it easier to keep track of your collection as it grows.

ADVANCING YOUR HOBBY

What next? There are many ways to take your hobby further, such as developing your collection, starting a project, or even making a career of it.

A SPECIALIST COLLECTION

With over 3,000 minerals, plus many types of rocks and fossils, most collectors soon decide to specialize in just one subject. For example, if you live in an area with good fossil deposits you might decide to build a collection of fossils. You can swap specimens with collectors from other areas, or buy from dealers, and you will probably find a section of the local museum or library that has useful references for study. Or you can specialize in the fossils of your local area, becoming an expert on the fossil deposits.

Some experts devote their time to a very specialist subject, seeking gemstones. Most people are familiar with gems such as diamond and sapphire; specialists look for gems that are uncommon in jewellery, or varieties of common gems that have unusual colours.

Collecting stamps that show rocks, fossils, minerals and dinosaurs can make an interesting sideline to your hobby.

PROJECTS

As well as organizing your main collection, why not start a simple project to do when you can't go collecting specimens? Here are a few ideas.

Build a collection of leaflets and advertisements which have details of caves and other interesting features. If you go on holiday in one of these areas, you'll have some useful background information before you arrive.

A survey of local road names will tell you a great deal about the geology of the surrounding area. Quarry Road and Brickpit Lane are probably common examples; Alum Lane might be a bit more unusual.

If you enjoy photography or drawing, why not make an album of the various rocks used in buildings, or the ways in which fossils have been used in designs for buildings, wallpaper and fabrics?

Make a survey of buildings, memorials and gravestones to find the rocks used to make them. Do *not* take samples from any of them! If you can't find the date on a building, look at old photographs or maps to estimate when they were built.

ADVANCED PROJECTS

You don't need to collect rocks and fossils to develop your hobby. Following the progress of a major road-building programme or gravel extraction in your area would make a good advanced project. Look in your local newspaper for news about road or quarrying schemes that you can study.

Ask the companies involved and your local authority for information and for permission to visit the site - perhaps on the day of a geological survey. As well as writing about your visit, take photographs or make maps and drawings to record what is happening. Why not write an article for your local paper, or see if you can present the project as part of your school work?

OPPORTUNITIES AT SCHOOL

Make the most of your opportunities at school. You might be able to explore other parts of the country on geology field trips, or visit museums more cheaply than going on your own. Schools will also organize work experience so you can find out more about the work of geologists employed by many industries, particularly oil, construction and water companies.

You may be able to think of other ways to develop your hobby. Whatever you do, have fun!

SOME USEFUL ADDRESSES

Australia: The Fossil Collecter's Association of Australia, 15 Kenbury Road, Heathmont, Victoria 3135, Australia.

Canada: The Geological Association of Canada, c/o Department of Earth Sciences, Memorial University of Newfoundland, St Johns, Newfoundland, A1B 3X5.

New Zealand: The Geological Society of New Zealand Inc, c/o New Zealand Geological Survey, Box 30-368, Lower Hutt, New Zealand.

United Kingdom: The Royal Society for Nature Conservation has set up RockWATCH, a club that will appeal to the whole family. Members get a magazine, membership card and programme of activities. For subscription details write to RockWATCH, The Green, Witham Park, Waterside South, Lincoln LN5 7JR.

United Kingdom: The Geologists' Association, Burlington House, Piccadilly, London W1.

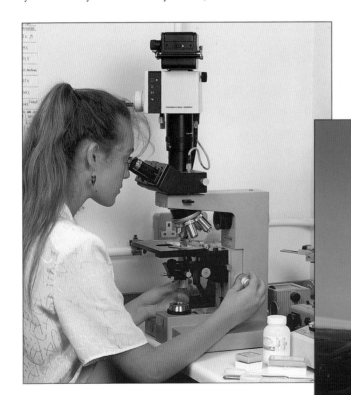

Some professional scientists and geologists (left) will have started their careers as a result of collecting rocks and fossils. The knowledge and skills you develop as part of your hobby could lead you into fascinating careers, such as using laser beams to monitor faults in earthquake zones (below).

INDEX

Italic figures refer to captions or to illustration labels.

acid, for tests *15*, 34
actinolite *65*
agate *41*, 69
albite *62*
algae 55
alum 62
aluminium *45*
aluminium oxide *67*
amber 50, *50*
amethyst 8, 32, 40, *40*, 70
ammonite *8*, 50, *50*, *52*
Andrews, Roy Chapman 56
Anning, Mary 56, *56*
anticline *24*, 31, *31*
apatite 33, *62*
aquamarine *70*
axinite *61*
azurite *47*

barite *61*
basalt *9*, 16, *16*, 17, 27
belemnite 50, *50*
beryl *60*
bloodstone *70*
borax bead test 37, *37*
breccia *18-19*, 27
bronze 44, *44*
bubble raft *60-61*

calcite 33, 34, *34*, 38, *38*, 39, *65*
calcium *36*
calcium carbonate 8, 42, 43, 62
carbon 68
cassiterite 39, 48
cast 52, *53*
cave 42, *42*, *43*, 47
chalcedony 69
chalk 8, *18*, 19, 27
chert 40, *41*
chromium *37*
chrysoprase *70*
citrine 32, 40, *40*, 69
clay 19, *19*
cleavage 32, 34
clinometer 31, *31*

coelacanth 57, *57*
compass *10*, 35
conglomerate *18*, 19, 27, *59*
copper *36*, *37*, 44, *45*, 48, 49, 62, *65*
coral *51*
cornelian *70*
corundum 33, 67, *67*
crinoid (sea lily) 51, *51*
crystal 8, 16, *16*, 60-67, *60-67*
Cuvier, Baron Georges 54

density 32, 35
diamond 33, 67, 68-9, *68*, *69*, *70*
dinosaur 56, *56-7*
    track 8, 52, *52*
dip, measuring 31, *31*

Earth *9*, 55
earthquake 24, 25, *25*
emerald *70*

fault 24, 25
feldspar 8, *8*, 17, 32, 39, *62*
flint 8, 19, 40, *41*, 69
fluorite *32*, 33, 38, 39
fold *19*, 24, *24*
fool's gold (pyrite) *47*, 47
foraminifera 59
fossil 8, *15*, 50-59
fossil forest *52-3*
froth flotation *49*

gabbro *16*, 17, 27
galena 38, 39, 67, *67*
garnet *22*, 39, *70*
Geiger counter 39, *39*
geode *41*
gneiss 22, *23*, 27
gold 48, *48*
grain size guide *26*
granite 8, *8*, 16, 17, 27, 28, 67
graphite 39, 68, *68*
gypsum 33, 38, 39, *61*

haematite *32*, *32*, 38, 39, 46
halite (rock salt) 34, 38, 39
hammering *11*

hardness, mineral 33
    water 43, *43*

ice 67, *67*
Ichthyosaurus 56, *56-7*
idocrase *60*
iron 9, 30, *45*, 46-7, 49, 67
Ironbridge *46*

jasper 40, *41*, 69

lapis lazuli *71*
lava 8, 16-17, *16-17*
Law of Superposition 54
limestone 18, *18-19*, 19, 22, 27, *28*, 34, 42, *42*
limonite 39, *46*, 47
lustre 32, 33

magma *9*, *17*
magnesium sulphate 62, *62*
magnetism 35
magnetite 38, 39, 46
malachite 38, 39
manganese 37
map 10, 30, *30-31*, 45
marble 22, *22*, 23, *23*, 27
marcasite *65*
metaquartzite *22*, *23*
meteorite 47
mica 8, *8*, 22, *22*, 34, 39
mica schist *22*
micraster 50
microfossil 59, *59*
mineral identification 38-9
Mohs scale 33
montmorillonite 32
moonstone *70*
mould 52
mountain 24
mudstone *18-19*, 19, 22, 27

nickel *9*, *37*, 47

obsidian *16*, 27, *34*, 41, *41*
oil 58-9, *59*
opal *71*
ore 44-6, 48-9, *49*
orthoclase 33
outcrop 31

panning 48, *48*
pearl *70*
pebble polishing 69, *69*
peridot *70*
pitchblende *39*
plate tectonics 55, *55*
potassium *36*
pterodactyl 54, *55*
pumice 17, *17*
pyrite *33*, 38, 39, 47, *47*, *60*
pyrophyllite *65*

quarry *29*

quartz 8, *8*, 27, 32, 33, 34, 38, 39, 40, *40*, 69

radioactivity 9
refraction 38, *38*
ripple mark 18, *20*
rock crystal *70*
rock cycle *23*
rock identification 27
ruby 64, *64*, *70*
rutile *65*

salt 20, *20*, 34, 66, *66*
sand 40, *40*
sand dollar *50*
sandstone 18, *18*, *19*, 27
sapphire *71*
sardonyx *70*
schist 22, *22*, *23*, 27
sea urchin 51, *51*
serpentine *33*
shale 22, 27
siderite *61*
sieving *12-13*
silica 40-41, 64, *64*, 67
slate 22, *22*, *23*, 27
smelting 44, 46
snowflake 67, *67*
sodalite *32*
sodium *36*
sodium thiosulphate 62
specimens, collecting 9, 26-9
    keeping *12-13*, 15, 72-3, *72-3*
    recording *11*, 13, 26, *26*
stalactite 42, *42*, *43*
stalagmite 42, *42*, *43*
stratigraphical table 54
stratum (*plural* strata) 18, *19*, 21, *21*, 31
streak test 32, *32*, 46
strike, measuring 31, *31*
strontium *36*
sugar crystal 8, *66*
sulphur 32, *32*, 39
surveying 30-31, *58-9*
syncline *24*, 31, *31*

talc 33, *33*, 39
tin 44, 48
tooth, shark *51*
topaz 33, *71*
tourmaline *71*
trilobite 51, *51*
tungsten *65*
turquoise *71*

volcano 8, *16-17*, 17, *23*, 24

willemite *38*
wolframite *65*

zinc 67
zircon 71, *71*

Once there was a
princess named Snow White.

5

Snow White's stepmother, the queen, was beautiful but very vain.

Snow White

by Maggie Moore and The Pope Twins

W
FRANKLIN WATTS
LONDON•SYDNEY

She always asked her magic mirror:
"Mirror, mirror on the wall,
who's the fairest of them all?"

Every time the mirror replied:
"Queen, you are the fairest in
the land."

As Snow White grew older,
she grew more beautiful.

Then one day, when the queen asked her mirror who was the fairest of all, she got a shock.

The mirror told her:
"Snow White is the fairest
in the land."

The queen was furious. She
ordered a huntsman to take
Snow White into the forest
and kill her.

But the kind huntsman felt sorry
for Snow White and let her go.

Snow White ran far into the forest and found a little house. Seven dwarfs lived there.

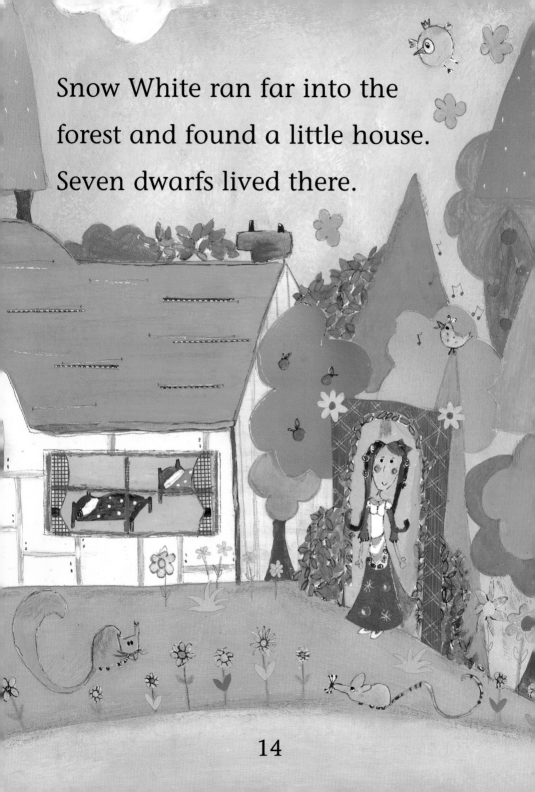

Snow White stayed and looked after the house while the dwarfs worked. They were all very happy.

One day, the queen asked her
mirror again who was the fairest.
"Snow White is the fairest in the
land," it still replied.

The queen realised that the
huntsman had tricked her.
She quickly sent her spies to
find Snow White.

When the queen found out where Snow White was hiding, she decided to get rid of Snow White herself.

First, she dressed up as an old woman and went to the little house to trick Snow White.

The queen tied ribbons so
tightly around Snow White's
waist that she could not breathe.

Luckily the dwarfs arrived
just in time to save her.

Next, the queen sold Snow White a poisoned comb and pushed it into her hair.

Again the dwarfs found her
before it was too late.

Finally, the queen tricked
Snow White into eating a
poisoned apple.

But this time the dwarfs were too
late. They put Snow White into
a glass case and looked after her.

The next day, a prince rode by and saw Snow White in the glass case. He thought she was the most beautiful girl he had ever seen.

He wanted to take Snow White
to his palace.

As the prince's men lifted Snow White from the case, the apple fell from her throat. She sat up and saw the prince.

They fell in love at once!

Snow White and the prince invited
the wicked queen to their wedding.
But the queen was so angry that
she ran away and was never
seen again.

Hopscotch has been specially designed to fit the requirements of the National Literacy Strategy. It offers real books by top authors and illustrators for children developing their reading skills. There are 43 Hopscotch stories to choose from:

Marvin, the Blue Pig
ISBN 978 0 7496 4619 6

Plip and Plop
ISBN 978 0 7496 4620 2

The Queen's Dragon
ISBN 978 0 7496 4618 9

Flora McQuack
ISBN 978 0 7496 4621 9

Willie the Whale
ISBN 978 0 7496 4623 3

Naughty Nancy
ISBN 978 0 7496 4622 6

Run!
ISBN 978 0 7496 4705 6

The Playground Snake
ISBN 978 0 7496 4706 3

"Sausages!"
ISBN 978 0 7496 4707 0

The Truth about Hansel and Gretel
ISBN 978 0 7496 4708 7

Pippin's Big Jump
ISBN 978 0 7496 4710 0

Whose Birthday Is It?
ISBN 978 0 7496 4709 4

The Princess and the Frog
ISBN 978 0 7496 5129 9

Flynn Flies High
ISBN 978 0 7496 5130 5

Clever Cat
ISBN 978 0 7496 5131 2

Moo!
ISBN 978 0 7496 5332 3

Izzie's Idea
ISBN 978 0 7496 5334 7

Roly-poly Rice Ball
ISBN 978 0 7496 5333 0

I Can't Stand It!
ISBN 978 0 7496 5765 9

Cockerel's Big Egg
ISBN 978 0 7496 5767 3

How to Teach a Dragon Manners
ISBN 978 0 7496 5873 1

The Truth about those Billy Goats
ISBN 978 0 7496 5766 6

Marlowe's Mum and the Tree House
ISBN 978 0 7496 5874 8

Bear in Town
ISBN 978 0 7496 5875 5

The Best Den Ever
ISBN 978 0 7496 5876 2

ADVENTURE STORIES

Aladdin and the Lamp
ISBN 978 0 7496 6678 1 *
ISBN 978 0 7496 6692 7

Blackbeard the Pirate
ISBN 978 0 7496 6676 7 *
ISBN 978 0 7496 6690 3

George and the Dragon
ISBN 978 0 7496 6677 4 *
ISBN 978 0 7496 6691 0

Jack the Giant-Killer
ISBN 978 0 7496 6680 4 *
ISBN 978 0 7496 6693 4

TALES OF KING ARTHUR

1. The Sword in the Stone
ISBN 978 0 7496 6681 1 *
ISBN 978 0 7496 6694 1

2. Arthur the King
ISBN 978 0 7496 6683 5 *
ISBN 978 0 7496 6695 8

3. The Round Table
ISBN 978 0 7496 6684 2 *
ISBN 978 0 7496 6697 2

4. Sir Lancelot and the Ice Castle
ISBN 978 0 7496 6685 9 *
ISBN 978 0 7496 6698 9

TALES OF ROBIN HOOD

Robin and the Knight
ISBN 978 0 7496 6686 6 *
ISBN 978 0 7496 6699 6

Robin and the Monk
ISBN 978 0 7496 6687 3 *
ISBN 978 0 7496 6700 9

Robin and the Friar
ISBN 978 0 7496 6688 0 *
ISBN 978 0 7496 6702 3

Robin and the Silver Arrow
ISBN 978 0 7496 6689 7 *
ISBN 978 0 7496 6703 0

FAIRY TALES

The Emperor's New Clothes
ISBN 978 0 7496 7077 1 *
ISBN 978 0 7496 7421 2

Cinderella
ISBN 978 0 7496 7073 3 *
ISBN 978 0 7496 7417 5

Snow White
ISBN 978 0 7496 7074 0 *
ISBN 978 0 7496 7418 2

Jack and the Beanstalk
ISBN 978 0 7496 7078 8 *
ISBN 978 0 7496 7422 9

The Three Billy Goats Gruff
ISBN 978 0 7496 7076 4 *
ISBN 978 0 7496 7420 5

The Pied Piper of Hamelin
ISBN 978 0 7496 7075 7 *
ISBN 978 0 7496 7419 9

* hardback